HISTORIC HOUSES**&** GARDENS

getmapping® + HarperCollins*Publishers*

HISTORIC HOUSES& GARDENS

100 AMAZING VIEWS FROM
www.getmapping**.com**

Contents

Althorp

Northampton, Northamptonshire

1. Built: 1508/1786
2. Family: Spencer
3. Architect: Henry Holland
   (1786 additions)
4. Built of: Red brick with stone
5. Features: Paintings by Gainsborough,
   Reynolds, Rubens, Van Dyck, Lely;
   Wootton Hall designed by Roger Morris
   & Colen Campbell
6. Gardens: Samuel Lappidge; André le
   Nôtre (reputedly)
7. Other: Haunted by a groom, a child and
   the 7th Earl; Wootton Hall was designed
   to house equestrian paintings by John
   Wootton, which exactly fill the walls

Owner: The Earl Spencer
Tel: (01604) 770107

The Spencer family was thrown into the limelight when Lady Diana
Spencer married the Prince of Wales in 1981, but the Spencers
have long been an influential, aristocratic dynasty. Since 1508
fifteen generations of Spencers have lived at Althorp, including five
knights, three Barons, five Earls of Sunderland, seven Earls
Spencer and one Duke of Marlborough, among those a Chief
Minister, a Secretary of State, a Leader of the House of Commons
and a Leader of the Liberal Peers.

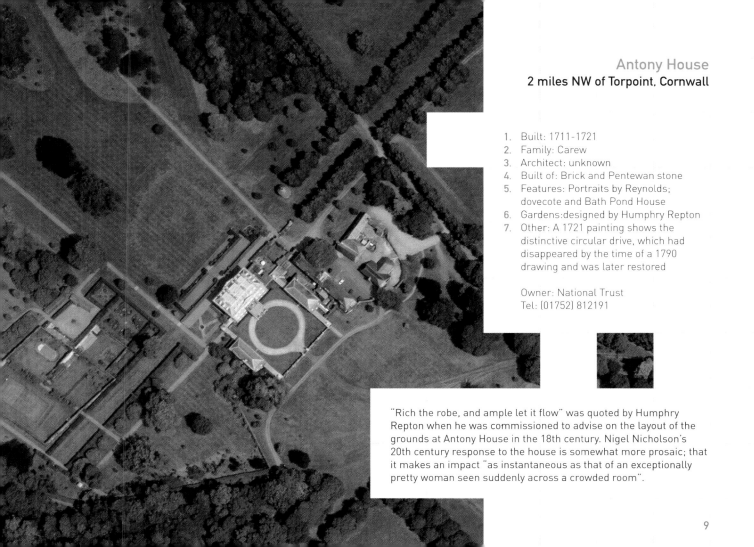

Antony House
2 miles NW of Torpoint, Cornwall

1. Built: 1711-1721
2. Family: Carew
3. Architect: unknown
4. Built of: Brick and Pentewan stone
5. Features: Portraits by Reynolds; dovecote and Bath Pond House
6. Gardens:designed by Humphry Repton
7. Other: A 1721 painting shows the distinctive circular drive, which had disappeared by the time of a 1790 drawing and was later restored

Owner: National Trust
Tel: (01752) 812191

"Rich the robe, and ample let it flow" was quoted by Humphry Repton when he was commissioned to advise on the layout of the grounds at Antony House in the 18th century. Nigel Nicholson's 20th century response to the house is somewhat more prosaic; that it makes an impact "as instantaneous as that of an exceptionally pretty woman seen suddenly across a crowded room".

Arlington Court
7 miles NE of Barnstaple, Devon

1. Built: 1822
2. Family: Chichester
3. Architect: Thomas Lee
4. Built of: Limestone block
5. Features: Collection of objets d'art; Blake's Cycle of the Life of Man
6. Other: When the National Trust took over the property the William Blake watercolour was discovered on top of a wardrobe

   Owner: National Trust
   Tel: (01271) 850296

Arlington Court was once the home of the Chichester family, whose most famous modern descendant is the yachtsman Sir Francis Chichester.

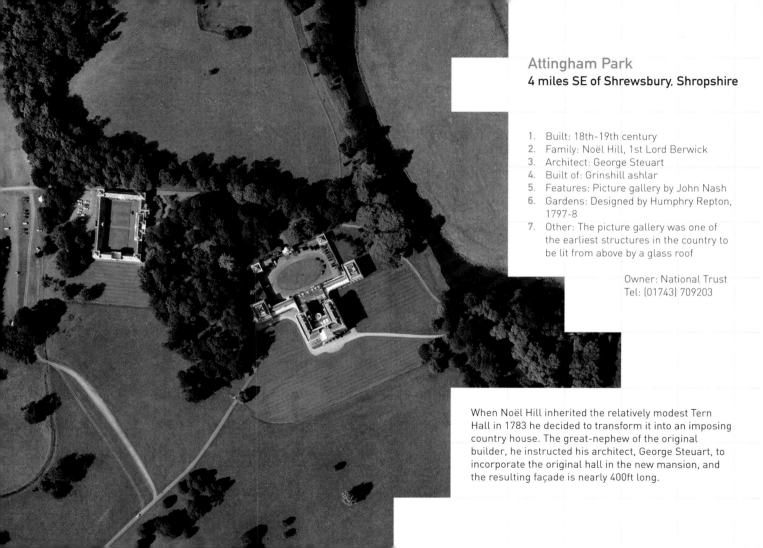

Attingham Park
4 miles SE of Shrewsbury, Shropshire

1. Built: 18th-19th century
2. Family: Noël Hill, 1st Lord Berwick
3. Architect: George Steuart
4. Built of: Grinshill ashlar
5. Features: Picture gallery by John Nash
6. Gardens: Designed by Humphry Repton, 1797-8
7. Other: The picture gallery was one of the earliest structures in the country to be lit from above by a glass roof

Owner: National Trust
Tel: (01743) 709203

When Noël Hill inherited the relatively modest Tern Hall in 1783 he decided to transform it into an imposing country house. The great-nephew of the original builder, he instructed his architect, George Steuart, to incorporate the original hall in the new mansion, and the resulting façade is nearly 400ft long.

Audley End House
1 mile W of Saffron Walden, Essex

1. Built: 17th century
2. Family: Howard/Braybrooke
3. Architect: for Thomas Howard, 1st Earl of Suffolk
4. Built of: Stone
5. Features: Braybrooke collection of pictures and furniture; natural history collection
6. Gardens: designed by Capability Brown
7. Other: requisitioned during World War II; the Kitchen Garden has been restored, including a 170ft long vinehouse; organic fruit, vegetables and flowers from the garden are sold on site

Owner: English Heritage
Tel: (01799) 522399

The 1st Earl of Suffolk was Lord Treasurer to James I and, in order to entertain his king, he built Audley End House on the scale of a royal palace - it later became one when it was bought for £50,000 by Charles II as a base when he attended the races at Newmarket. The house returned to the Suffolks in 1701 and, unusually, has since been reduced in size, with demolitions of the main front court and the east wing in 1708 and 1753.

Bagshot Park
Bagshot, Surrey

1. Built: 1879/1997-2000
2. Family: Crown
3. Architect: Stephen Batchelor (20thC)
4. Built of: Red brick
5. Features: Chapel, bell tower, Indian sandalwood billiard room
6. Gardens: 87 acres of parkland
7. Other: The wrought iron gates, valued at £100,000, were stolen in 1990 and later found in a local scrap yard; the former stable block at Bagshot Park is now the home of Edward Wessex's television production company, Ardent Productions

Owner: Crown
Tel: private

Queen Victoria had Bagshot Park rebuilt during the late 19th century for her third son Prince Arthur, Duke of Connaught, but Bagshot's royal connections go back much further than that – a royal hunting lodge in the park was a favourite of the Stuart kings. History repeated itself at the end of the 20th century when a monarch's third son again took up residence; this time it was the Earl of Wessex, better known as Prince Edward, who moved in with his bride Sophie Rhys-Jones.

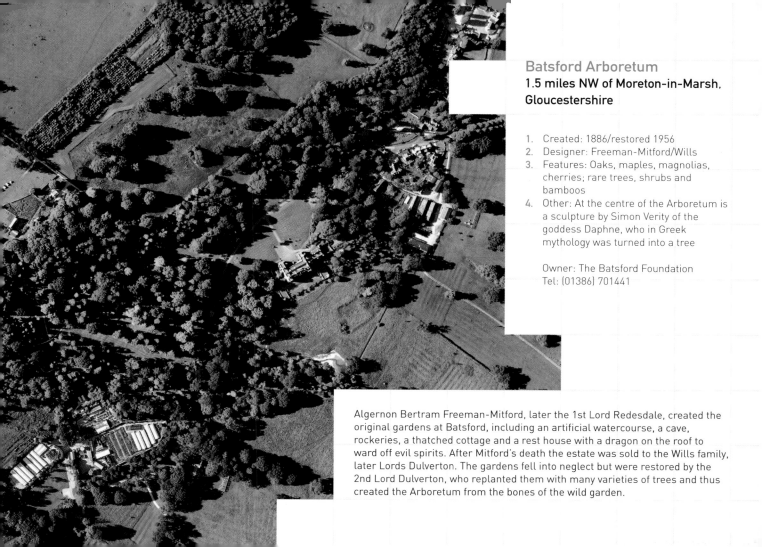

Batsford Arboretum
1.5 miles NW of Moreton-in-Marsh, Gloucestershire

1. Created: 1886/restored 1956
2. Designer: Freeman-Mitford/Wills
3. Features: Oaks, maples, magnolias, cherries; rare trees, shrubs and bamboos
4. Other: At the centre of the Arboretum is a sculpture by Simon Verity of the goddess Daphne, who in Greek mythology was turned into a tree

Owner: The Batsford Foundation
Tel: (01386) 701441

Algernon Bertram Freeman-Mitford, later the 1st Lord Redesdale, created the original gardens at Batsford, including an artificial watercourse, a cave, rockeries, a thatched cottage and a rest house with a dragon on the roof to ward off evil spirits. After Mitford's death the estate was sold to the Wills family, later Lords Dulverton. The gardens fell into neglect but were restored by the 2nd Lord Dulverton, who replanted them with many varieties of trees and thus created the Arboretum from the bones of the wild garden.

Belton House
3 miles NE of Grantham, Lincolnshire

1. Built: 1684-7
2. Family: Brownlow
3. Architect: Unknown/altered by James Wyatt during the 1770s
4. Built of: Ashlar from Ancaster quarry
5. Features: Family portraits by Reynolds; plasterwork ceilings by Edward Goudge
6. Other: Belton House closely follows the design of Clarendon House in Piccadilly, demolished the year Belton was begun

Owner: National Trust
Tel: (01476) 566116

Sir John Brownlow has no statue among the family memorials in the church at Belton, because "the testimony of his noble house which he built from the ground" was considered a sufficient monument. It is said that his five daughters were giving an unsanctioned tea-party upstairs at Belton when they heard footsteps approaching, and that in order to avoid detection they threw the entire tea-service out of the window.

Beningbrough Hall
8 miles NW of York, North Yorkshire

1. Built: 1716
2. Family: Bourchier
3. Architect: Uncertain, possibly Thomas Archer
4. Built of: Red brick dressed with stone
5. Features: Permanent exhibition of 100 paintings from the National Portrait Gallery; cantilevered staircase with treads 7ft wide
6. Other: The central window above the entrance is copied from a window by Bernini in Rome

Owner: National Trust
Tel: (01904) 470666

Sir John Bourchier, who owned Beningbrough at the time of the Civil War, was among those who passed sentence on Charles I and it is remarkable that his heirs retained the estate after the Restoration. The silver seal that Bourchier impressed on the king's death warrant is preserved in the present Beningbrough Hall, which was built for his grandson, another John Bourchier.

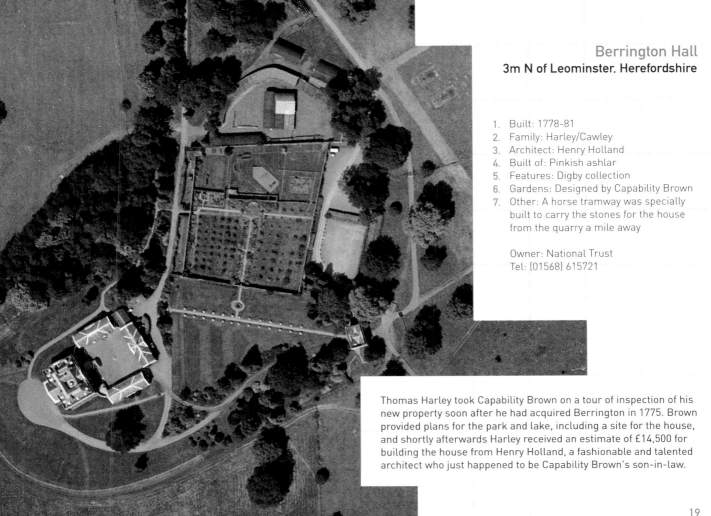

Berrington Hall
3m N of Leominster, Herefordshire

1. Built: 1778-81
2. Family: Harley/Cawley
3. Architect: Henry Holland
4. Built of: Pinkish ashlar
5. Features: Digby collection
6. Gardens: Designed by Capability Brown
7. Other: A horse tramway was specially built to carry the stones for the house from the quarry a mile away

Owner: National Trust
Tel: (01568) 615721

Thomas Harley took Capability Brown on a tour of inspection of his new property soon after he had acquired Berrington in 1775. Brown provided plans for the park and lake, including a site for the house, and shortly afterwards Harley received an estimate of £14,500 for building the house from Henry Holland, a fashionable and talented architect who just happened to be Capability Brown's son-in-law.

Bicton Park Botanical Gardens
2 miles N of Budleigh Salterton, Devon

1. Created: Early 18th century
2. Designer: Henry, 1st Baron Rolle
3. Features: House of Shells; secret garden; the Palm House, an 1820 conservatory comprising 18,000 separate pieces of glass
4. Other: The gardens include fountains, water features, sweeping lawns, formal gardens and English borders

Owner: Simon & Valerie Lister
Tel: (01395) 568465

The Grade I Listed Gardens at Bicton Park boast a remarkable Palm House pre-dating the one at Kew by twenty years, an Italian Garden by André le Nôtre, who planned Louis XIV's gardens at the Palace of Versailles, and the narrow gauge Bicton Woodland Railway which transports visitors on a twenty-five minute journey through the grounds.

Blenheim Palace
Woodstock, Oxfordshire

1. Built: 1705-20
2. Family: Churchill, Dukes of Marlborough
3. Architect: Sir John Vanbrugh
4. Built of: Honey-coloured stone
5. Features: Portraits by Reynolds and Sargent; Hawksmoor library; carvings by Grinling Gibbons; Thornhill ceiling
6. Gardens: 2,100 acres designed by Capability Brown
7. Other: Winston Churchill was born here in 1874; location for Kenneth Branagh's Hamlet; Vanbrugh was also the architect of Castle Howard

Phone: 01993 811091
Ownership: 11th Duke of Marlborough

Blenheim Palace was built as a gift from Queen Anne and the nation to John Churchill, the 1st Duke of Marlborough, to commemorate his victories over the French, and the house is named after his most famous battle. Previously known as Blenheim House and Blenheim Castle, it is the only Palace in England that is not royal or episcopal.

Blickling Hall
1.5 miles NW of Aylsham, Norfolk

1. Built: 1616-25
2. Family: Hobart/Lothian
3. Architect: Robert Lyminge
4. Built of: Red brick
5. Features: A tapestry that was a gift from Catherine the Great; interiors by Thomas and William Ivory
6. Gardens: Designed by John Adey Repton; mausoleum by Bonomi
7. Other: Haunted by Anne Boleyn and a coach drawn by headless horses

Owner: National Trust
Tel: (01263) 738030

The Blickling estate was at one time owned by the Boleyn family, and it is said that Anne Boleyn was born and grew up in an earlier house on the site – it is also said that she haunts the existing one. The present Blickling Hall was built for Lord Chief Justice Sir Henry Hobart, and later passed to the Earls of Buckingham.

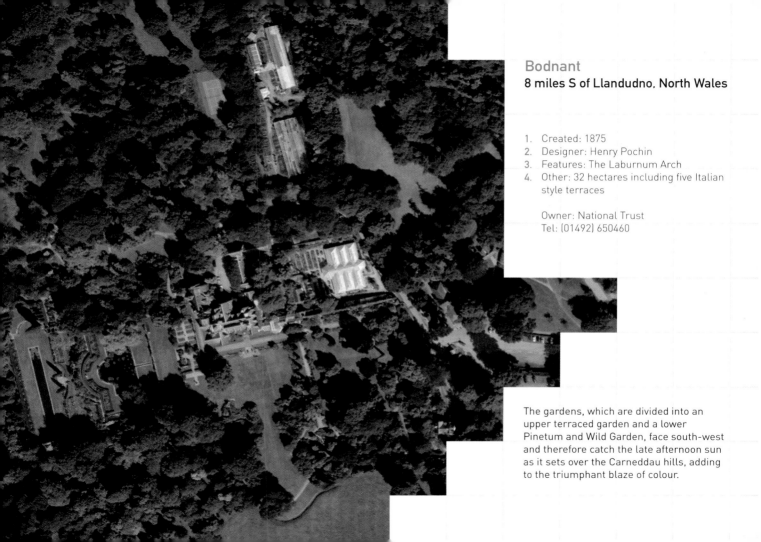

Bodnant
8 miles S of Llandudno, North Wales

1. Created: 1875
2. Designer: Henry Pochin
3. Features: The Laburnum Arch
4. Other: 32 hectares including five Italian style terraces

   Owner: National Trust
   Tel: (01492) 650460

The gardens, which are divided into an upper terraced garden and a lower Pinetum and Wild Garden, face south-west and therefore catch the late afternoon sun as it sets over the Carneddau hills, adding to the triumphant blaze of colour.

Boughton House
3 miles N of Kettering, Northamptonshire

1. Built: 1528/1688-1709
2. Family: Montagu/Buccleuch
3. Architect: For Ralph, 3rd Lord Montagu
4. Built of: Stone
5. Features: Buccleuch Collection including El Greco, Murillo and over forty Van Dycks; friezes and ceilings by Louis Chéron
6. Gardens: Designed by the 1st and 2nd Dukes of Montagu; the 2nd Duke is said to have planted seventy miles of lime and elm
7. Other: The large number of Mortlake tapestries may be connected with Lord Montagu buying the factory in 1674

Owner `: Duke of Buccleuch
Tel: (01536) 515731

Known when it was built as "The English Versailles", Boughton House incorporates a 500 year-old Tudor Monastic building, the ancestral home of the Montagus. The design was inspired by Lord Montagu's visits as ambassador to the court of Louis XIV

Broadlands
Romsey, Hampshire

1. Built: 16th/18th century
2. Family: Palmerston/Mountbatten
3. Architect: Brown/Holland (both 18thC)
4. Built of: Faced with yellow-grey brick
5. Features: Wedgwood china; paintings by Van Dyck; Palmerston collection; plasterwork by Joseph Rose
6. Gardens: Designed by Capability Brown, 1766
7. Other: Houses a Mountbatten exhibition; now home to Mountbatten's grandson Lord Romsey

Owner: Lord Romsey
Tel: (01794) 505010

Her Majesty The Queen and Prince Philip, now Duke of Edinburgh, spent part of their honeymoon at Broadlands in 1947 when it was still the home of Lord Mountbatten.

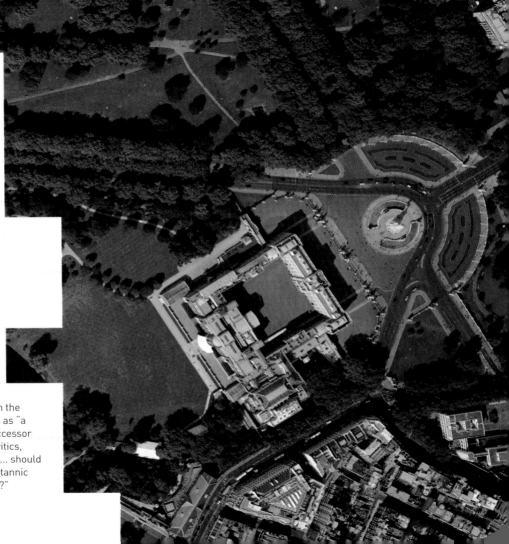

Buckingham Palace
London SW1

1. Built: 1702-5/1820-37
2. Family: Crown
3. Architect: Winde/Nash/Blore
4. Built of: Portland stone façade
5. Features: Gobelin tapestries; paintings by Van Dyck, Rembrandt, Vermeer; picture gallery by John Nash
6. Other: Haunted by a monk; in 1837 Queen Victoria became the first monarch to make Buckingham Palace her official residence

Owner: Crown
Tel: (020) 7839 1377

Architect John Nash was criticized for a dome on the palace roof, later removed, which was described as "a common slop pail turned upside down" – his successor Edward Blore didn't fare much better with the critics, who asked in 1832: "Is it possible that the nation... should provide for the metropolitan residence of His Britannic Majesty such a gimcrack as Buckingham House?"

Burghley House
Stamford, Lincolnshire

1. Built: 1555-87
2. Family: Cecil
3. Architect: William Cecil
4. Built of: Mellow ragstone
5. Features: Pyramidal clocktower; ceilings by Antonio Verrio and Louis Laguerre
6. Gardens: Designed by Capability Brown
7. Other: William Cecil was chief minister to Elizabeth I for forty years

Owner: Burghley House Preservation Trust Ltd
Tel: (01780) 752451

Elizabeth I was right when she said of William Cecil, the builder of Burghley House, that "you will not be corrupted with any manner of gifts, and will remain faithful to the state". As Chief Secretary of State he successfully steered his Queen through many political difficulties, from the wars against Spain to the execution of Mary, Queen of Scots.

Buscot Park
2 miles SE of Lechlade, Oxfordshire

1. Built: c1780
2. Family: Lord Faringdon
3. Architect: Edward Loveden Townsend
4. Built of: Stone
5. Features: Faringdon collection including paintings by Reynolds, Gainsborough, Rembrandt and Murillo
6. Gardens: Designed by Harold Peto in the 20th century
7. Other: In the 16th century the manor belonged to the Stonors of Oxfordshire who also owned Stonor Park

Owner: National Trust
Tel: 0845 3453387

Robert Campbell, an Australian gold trader, bought Buscot in 1859 and proceeded with a programme of agricultural industrialization that included irrigation schemes and a narrow-gauge railway running round the estate. He also built a distillery on an island in the Thames for making spirit from sugar beet – the island is still known as Brandy Island.

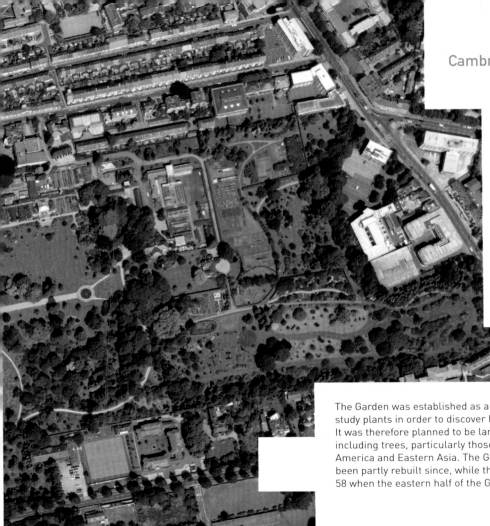

Cambridge University Botanic Gardens
Cambridge, Cambridgeshire

1. Created: 1846
2. Designer: Professor John Stevens Henslow
3. Features: Collections of trees and shrubs, botanical groups of herbaceous perennials; lake
4. Other: Founded in 1762 and transferred to the present site in 1846, the gardens cover 40 acres

Owner: Cambridge University
Tel: (01223) 336265

The Garden was established as a University teaching and research resource to study plants in order to discover how they worked and how they could be used. It was therefore planned to be large enough to accommodate many species, including trees, particularly those which were then being discovered in North America and Eastern Asia. The Glasshouse Range dates from 1880-89, but has been partly rebuilt since, while the Limestone Rock Garden was added in 1954-58 when the eastern half of the Garden was also being developed.

Castle Drogo
Drewsteignton, Devon

1. Built: 1910-1930
2. Family: Drewe
3. Architect: Sir Edwin Lutyens
4. Built of: Local granite
5. Features: Has its own hydro-electric and telephone systems
6. Other: Julius Drewe, for whom Castle Drogo was built, launched the business that became known as The Home and Colonial Stores

Owner: National Trust
Tel: (01647) 433306

Grocery magnate Julius Drewe retired at the age of 33 and discovered a tenuous family link with a Norman baron, so he set about building a castle befitting his new-found nobility. Built on land once owned by his putative ancestors, the castle is named after them – the Drogos, or Drus, whose name is preserved in the near-by village of Drewsteignton.

Castle Howard Estate
15 miles NE of York, North Yorkshire

1. Built: 18th century
2. Family: Howard, Earls of Carlisle
3. Architect: Sir John Vanbrugh
4. Built of: Local stone
5. Features: Paintings by Holbein, Rubens, Gainsborough, Reynolds; chapel with stained glass by Edward Burne-Jones
6. Gardens: 1000 acres by Vanburgh, including the Temple of the Four Winds
7. Other: Location for Brideshead Revisited; the Howard family mausoleum was designed by Hawksmoor and is taller than the house itself

Owner: Honourable Simon Howard
Tel: (01653) 648333

When he started building Castle Howard, architect John Vanbrugh was better known as a playwright and, having no formal architectural training, he asked Nicholas Hawksmoor to assist him with the structural elements. Castle Howard was such a success that one wit of the time wrote: "Van's genius, without thought or lecture/ Is hugely turned to architecture" and the two went on to work together on Blenheim Palace.

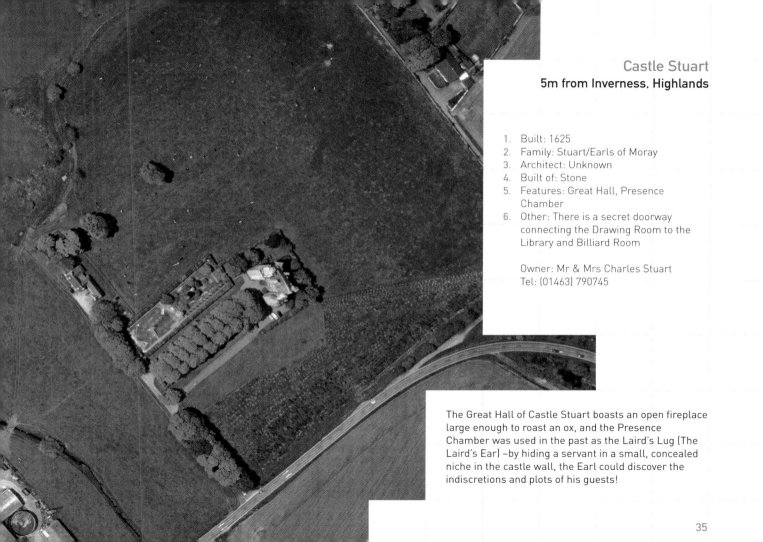

Castle Stuart
5m from Inverness, Highlands

1. Built: 1625
2. Family: Stuart/Earls of Moray
3. Architect: Unknown
4. Built of: Stone
5. Features: Great Hall, Presence Chamber
6. Other: There is a secret doorway connecting the Drawing Room to the Library and Billiard Room

Owner: Mr & Mrs Charles Stuart
Tel: (01463) 790745

The Great Hall of Castle Stuart boasts an open fireplace large enough to roast an ox, and the Presence Chamber was used in the past as the Laird's Lug (The Laird's Ear) –by hiding a servant in a small, concealed niche in the castle wall, the Earl could discover the indiscretions and plots of his guests!

35

Charlecote Park
5 miles E of Stratford, Warwickshire

1. Built: c1558/19th century
2. Family: Lucy
3. Architect: Sir Thomas Lucy
4. Built of: Red brick
5. Features: Interiors by Thomas Willemont
6. Gardens: Designed by Capability Brown, who was commissioned c1760 for £525
7. Other: Charles I camped in the meadow before Battle of Edgehill in 1642; Sir Thomas Lucy entertained Elizabeth I to breakfast here during her summer 1572 progress to Kenilworth

Owner: National Trust
Tel: (01789) 470277

It is said that Sir Thomas Lucy once fined a young poet for poaching in the deer park at Charlecote, and that the poet later ridiculed Sir Thomas in his plays. The latter part at least is true, because Sir Thomas, who was a magistrate, served as a model for Justice Shallow in Shakespeare's Henry IV, Part Two and The Merry Wives of Windsor - Shakespeare even mentions a "dozen white luces" in the knight's coat of arms, a pun on the Lucy family name.

Chatsworth

9 miles N of Matlock, Derbyshire

1. Built: 1686-1707
2. Family: Cavendish, Dukes of Devonshire
3. Architect: Talman/Archer/Wyattville
4. Built of: Golden-yellow stone
5. Features: Private collection; ceilings by Louis Laguerre
6. Gardens: Designed by Capability Brown/Wyattville/Paxton
7. Other: Paxton's Emperor Fountain was once the world's highest gravity-fed fountain but now reaches only 100ft

Owner: Duke of Devonshire
Tel: (01246) 582204

Chatsworth was built by William Cavendish despite the twin financial difficulties of his addiction to horseracing and a massive fine he owed for tweaking the nose of one of James II's courtiers. The fine was waived in 1689 after Cavendish and his allies had ousted James II and replaced him with William of Orange in the "Glorious Revolution", and by the time Chatsworth was completed Cavendish had been made 1st Duke of Devonshire.

Chequers
Great Missenden, Buckinghamshire

1. Built: 1565/restored 1892-c1909
2. Family: Hawtrey/Lee
3. Architect: for William Hawtrey/restored by Reginald Blomfield
4. Built of: Red brick with stone mullions
5. Features: Collection of Cromwell memorabilia; Long Gallery with a secret door lined with dummy books leading to the Cromwell Corridor
6. Gardens: 300 acres improved by Reginald Blomfield; rose garden with a caption engraved in stone above the entrance: "All care abandon ye who enter here"
7. Other: Lady Mary Grey, sister of Lady Jane Grey the "nine days' queen", was imprisoned at Chequers

Owner: HM Government

The January 1909 edition of Country Life described Chequers as a "beautiful old house with many historic associations... approached by two drives with entrance lodges". That was the year that Arthur Lee, Conservative MP for Fareham, saw the house and bought the lease. Lee was able to buy the freehold in 1917, and in that same year he arranged to bequeath Chequers to the nation as the official country residence of successive Prime Ministers

Chiswick House
Chiswick, London W4

1. Built: 1720s
2. Family: Burlington
3. Architect: 3rd Earl of Burlington
4. Built of: Stone
5. Features: William Kent interiors, including the Blue Velvet Room
6. Gardens: Italianate gardens designed by William Kent, with statues, temples, urns and obelisks
7. Other: The octagonal domed Saloon is lit by drum windows inspired by the Roman baths of Diocletian

Owner: English Heritage
Tel: (020) 8995 0508

Like Palladio's Villa Rotonda near Vicenza that inspired it, Chiswick house was built as a "temple to the arts". As well as charging visitors an admission fee to view his collection, Lord Burlington would entertain his friends here, including Swift, Handel and Alexander Pope who lived nearby in Twickenham.

Claydon House
Middle Claydon, Buckinghamshire

1. Built: 1754
2. Family: Verney
3. Architect: 2nd Earl Verney
4. Built of: Limestone, with a brick-built Victorian wing
5. Features: Carvings by Luke Lightfoot; Chinese room; ceiling by Joseph Rose
6. Other: Parthenope Verney was the elder sister of Florence Nightingale

Owner: National Trust
Tel: (01296) 730349

Sir Edmund Verney, who built Claydon, chose to remain loyal to Charles I during the Civil War despite being convinced that the Parliamentary cause was right. He was made Standard Bearer to the king, and, although his body was never recovered after the Battle of Edgehill, his severed hand was found still clutching the royal standard.

41

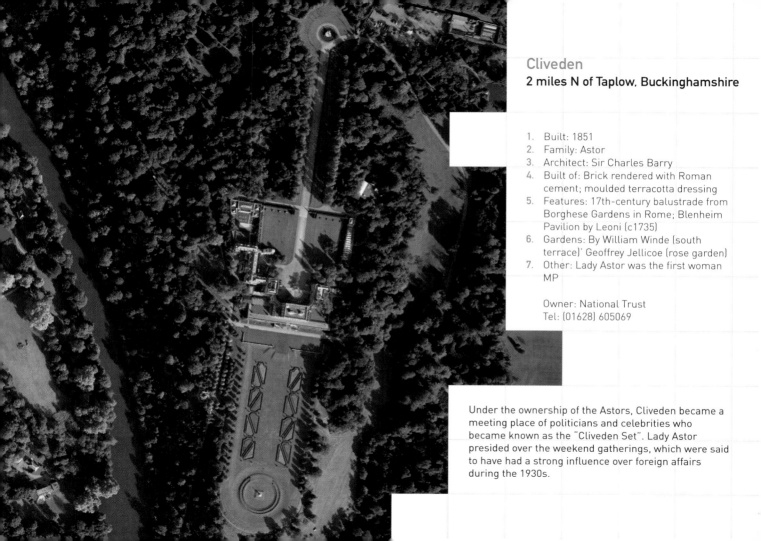

Cliveden
2 miles N of Taplow, Buckinghamshire

1. Built: 1851
2. Family: Astor
3. Architect: Sir Charles Barry
4. Built of: Brick rendered with Roman cement; moulded terracotta dressing
5. Features: 17th-century balustrade from Borghese Gardens in Rome; Blenheim Pavilion by Leoni (c1735)
6. Gardens: By William Winde (south terrace)' Geoffrey Jellicoe (rose garden)
7. Other: Lady Astor was the first woman MP

Owner: National Trust
Tel: (01628) 605069

Under the ownership of the Astors, Cliveden became a meeting place of politicians and celebrities who became known as the "Cliveden Set". Lady Astor presided over the weekend gatherings, which were said to have had a strong influence over foreign affairs during the 1930s.

Cotehele
2 miles E of St Dominick Cornwall

1. Built: 1485
2. Family: Edgcumbe
3. Architect: Richard & Piers Edgcumbe
4. Built of: Granite
5.. Features: 1480s pre-pendulum clock that still works
6. Gardens: The estate includes a watermill and a quay on the River Tamar
7. Other: The Edgcumbes had left by the end of the 18th century and tourists, including George III, began to visit Cotehele

Owner: National Trust
Tel: (01579) 351346

Cornwall was a lawless place in the 15th century, and Richard Edgcumbe built a house that was to survive an attempt by his feuding neighbour to burn it down. Edgcumbe was subsequently besieged at Cotehele by representatives of Richard III, and escaped by running to the river and throwing his hat into the water – his pursuers thought he had drowned. He then joined Henry Tudor in France, and was knighted after Henry defeated Richard III at the Battle of Bosworth to become King Henry VII.

Coughton Court
2 miles N of Alcester, Warwickshire

1. Built: 1530/18th century
2. Family: Throckmorton
3. Architect: Sir George Throckmorton
4. Built of: Stone
5. Features: The dress worn by Mary Queen of Scots at her execution; priestholes
6. Other: Attacked by both Parliamentarians and Royalists in the Civil War; supporters of the Gunpowder Plot and wives of the conspirators waited here for news of the outcome

Owner: National Trust
Tel: (01789) 4007777

A 17th-century historian describes "that stately castle-like Gatehouse of freestone" at Coughton Court, but implies that the rest of the house does not live up to it by asserting that Sir George Throckmorton had intended "to have made the rest of his house suitable thereto".

Ditchley Park
2.5 miles NE of Charlbury, Oxfordshire

1. Built: 1720s
2. Family: Lee, Earl of Lichfield/Dillon
3. Architect: James Gibbs
4. Built of: Burford stone
5. Features: Interiors by William Kent and Henry Flitcroft
6. Other: Used by Churchill from 1940-42 when Chequers was under threat of attack; now used as an Anglo-American conference centre

Owner: The Ditchley Foundation
Tel: (01608) 677346

Ditchley Park stands on the site of an earlier building used by James I when hunting in Wychwood Forest, which in medieval times was as large as the New Forest is now. The house was later owned by the ancestors of General Robert E Lee, who fought for the South in the American Civil War.

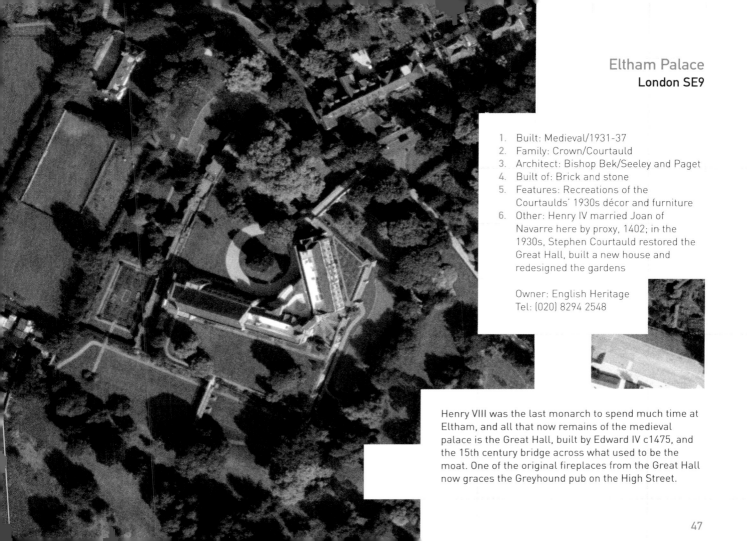

Eltham Palace
London SE9

1. Built: Medieval/1931-37
2. Family: Crown/Courtauld
3. Architect: Bishop Bek/Seeley and Paget
4. Built of: Brick and stone
5. Features: Recreations of the Courtaulds' 1930s décor and furniture
6. Other: Henry IV married Joan of Navarre here by proxy, 1402; in the 1930s, Stephen Courtauld restored the Great Hall, built a new house and redesigned the gardens

Owner: English Heritage
Tel: (020) 8294 2548

Henry VIII was the last monarch to spend much time at Eltham, and all that now remains of the medieval palace is the Great Hall, built by Edward IV c1475, and the 15th century bridge across what used to be the moat. One of the original fireplaces from the Great Hall now graces the Greyhound pub on the High Street.

Erddig
2 miles S of Wrexham, North Wales

1. Built: 1680s/18th century
2. Family: Meller/Yorke
3. Architect: Thomas Webb/James Wyatt
4. Built of: Brick, later stone-faced
5. Features: State bed in Chinese silk;
   portrait of Yorke by Gainsborough;
   circular waterfall known as The Cup
   and Saucer
6. Gardens: Designed by William Emes
7. Other: Contains the National Ivy
   Collection

Owner: National Trust
Tel: (01978) 355314

Erdigg was almost destroyed by subsidence
from coal mining but the National Trust
managed to save the hall using
compensation from the Coal Board
together with money raised by selling 64
acres of the park to the town of Wrexham.

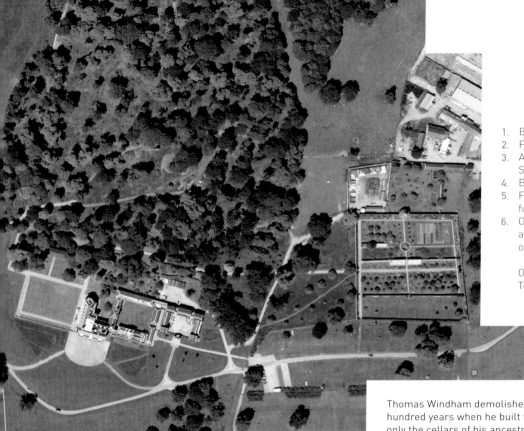

Felbrigg Hall
2 miles SW of Cromer, Norfolk

1. Built: 1620/1675-86
2. Family: Windham
3. Architect: Thomas Windham/William Samwell
4. Built of: Brick, stone & flint
5. Features: Collection of 18th century furniture; portraits by Lely
6. Other: Unusual L-shape design in two architectural styles, one Jacobean the other Charles II

Owner: National Trust
Tel: (01263) 837444

Thomas Windham demolished the family mansion of nearly two hundred years when he built the first part of Felbrigg Hall, keeping only the cellars of his ancestral home. His son William was less radical when he built his classical wing only sixty years later, simply erecting it at right-angles to the existing wing – the two are close in space and time but worlds apart in terms of architectural style.

Gardens of the Rose
Chiswell Green, 2 miles S of St Albans, Hertfordshire

1. Created: 1959-63
2. Designer: HG Clacy, then Vice-President RNRS
3. Features: Over 30,000 rose plants of 1,650 different varieties
4. Other: Gardens include the International Trial Ground for new roses

   Owner: Royal National Rose Society
   Tel: (01727) 850461

Officially called the Royal National Rose Garden, the Gardens of the Rose were opened in 1963 by the Royal National Rose Society's then Patron Princess Mary, The Princess Royal. The gardens are about to be extended to some 65 acres.

Haddon Hall
1.5 miles S of Bakewell, Derbyshire

1. Built: Medieval
2. Family: Vernon/Manners
3. Architect: For Avenell
4. Built of: Gritstone/limestone/oak
5. Features: 110ft Long Gallery panelled in oak & walnut
6. Other: The gardens appeared as Mr Rochester's Thornfield in Zeffirelli's Jane Eyre; the hall was abandoned by the Manners family in 1700 but restored from 1912 by 9th Duke of Rutland

Owner: Lord Edward Manners
Tel: (01629) 812855

For eight-and-a-half centuries Haddon Hall has remained in the hands of two families, linked by a marriage which is commemorated on a joint tomb in nearby Bakewell church. In the 12th century the Hall passed to the Vernons from its Norman founders the Avenells, and four hundred years later the sole heir, Dorothy Vernon, married John Manners, whose family later became Dukes of Rutland and who still own Haddon Hall.

Ham House
Richmond, Surrey

1. Built: 1610
2. Family: Duke of Lauderdale
3. Architect: For Sir Thomas Vavasour
4. Built of: Red brick with stone dressing
5. Features: portraits by Lely, Delft vases, K'ang-Hsi porcelain; ceiling by Verrio
6. Other: Haunted by the Duchess of Lauderdale; Evelyn visited in 1678 and was taken by the layout of the gardens

Owner: National Trust
Tel: (020) 8940 1950

Ham House is a rich, sumptuous, ornately decorated house created by the Duke and Duchess of Lauderdale, who have been described as being "among the least attractive couples of their age". Lady Dysart was "violently ambitious" and "of a most ravenous covetousness", while Lauderdale was "the coldest friend and the most violent enemy that ever was known".

Hampton Court Palace
Surrey KT8

1. Built: Tudor/17th century
2. Family: Wolsey/Crown
3. Architect: Remodelled by Wren
4. Built of: Red brick
5. Features: State Apartments; Tudor kitchens; maze and Tudor real tennis court
6. Other: Edward VI was born here on 12th October 1537; haunted by Anne Boleyn, Catherine Howard and Sibell Penn, nurse to Edward VI

Owner: Historic Royal Palaces
Tel: (020) 8781 9500

Thomas Wolsey, Cardinal and Lord Chancellor, built at Hampton Court a building of such splendour that Henry VIII was prompted to ask why. Wolsey reputedly replied, "To show how noble a place a subject may offer his sovereign" – prophetic words indeed, because when Wolsey fell from favour Henry took possession of Hampton Court and extended it still further for his own use.

Hanbury Hall
4.5 miles E of Droitwich, Worcestershire

1. Built: 1701
2. Family: Vernon
3. Architect: William Rudhall
4. Built of: Red brick
5. Features: Watney collection of porcelain; painted ceilings & staircase by Thornhill
6. Gardens: 18th-century garden (restored 1993) with parterre, bowling green and the original orangery
7. Other: Thomas Vernon, for whom Hanbury Hall was built, was a barrister and MP for the City of Worcester

Owner: National Trust
Tel: (01527) 821214

Thornhill's murals at Hanbury Hall include the expected scenes from classical mythology but also a surprising reference to the news of the day – a depiction of Dr Sacheverell being torn by the Furies. In 1710 the doctor was tried and found guilty of preaching a seditious sermon and the painting was commissioned soon afterwards.

Hardwick Hall
9.5 miles SE of Chesterfield, Derbyshire

1. Built: 1591-97
2. Family: Shrewsbury
3. Architect: Elizabeth Shrewsbury/Robert Smythson
4. Built of: Stone
5. Features: Needlework by Mary, Queen of Scots; High Great Chamber and Long Gallery
6. Other: Mary Queen of Scots was held prisoner here; Hardwick's many windows gave rise to the couplet "Hardwick Hall, more glass than wall".

Owner: National Trust
Tel: (01246) 850430

Elizabeth Shrewsbury, better known as Bess of Hardwick, was already well known for building houses when she began work on Hardwick at the age of 70. The Hall is famous for its windows, which would have been an expression of wealth in the 16th century when glass was still extremely expensive - but Bess was in a good position to demand so many windows, because she also owned a glassworks.

Harewood House
Harewood, West Yorkshire

1. Built: 1759-1771
2. Family: Harewood
3. Architect: John Carr/Robert Adam
4. Built of: Local limestone
5. Features: Paintings by Turner, Reynolds, Gainsborough, El Greco, Romsey; Chippendale furniture; plasterwork by Joseph Rose
6. Gardens: Designed by Capability Brown, 1772
7. Other: The house has inspired watercolours by Turner, Girtin and John Varley

Owner: Earl and Countess of Harewood
Tel: (0113) 218 1010

Sir George Henry Hubert Lascelles, 7th Earl of Harewood and elder son of the Queen's cousin, is better known to the cinema-going public simply as "Harewood", familiar from his signature during eleven years as president of the British Board of Film Classification.

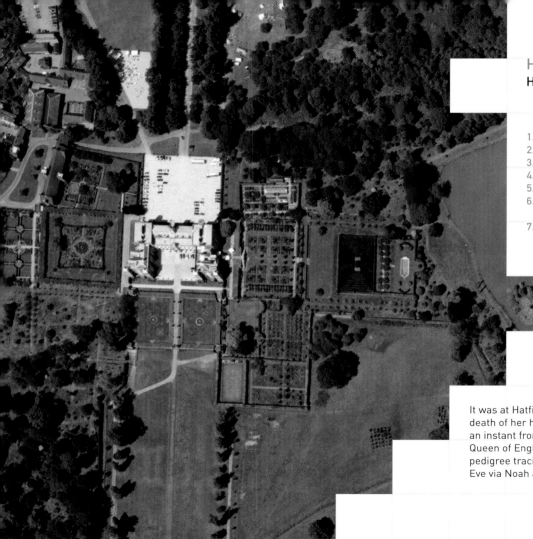

Hatfield House
Hatfield, Hertfordshire

1. Built: 1607-11
2. Family: Cecil
3. Architect: Robert Cecil
4. Built of: Red brick
5. Features: Elizabeth I's silk stockings
6. Gardens: Formal gardens designed by John Tradescant
7. Other: Childhood home of Elizabeth I; James I disliked Hatfield, and swapped it with his Chief Minister Sir Robert Cecil for Theobalds

Owner: Marquess of Salisbury
Tel: (01707) 287010

It was at Hatfield that Elizabeth I heard news of the death of her half-sister Mary, which transformed her in an instant from a semi-prisoner in her own home to Queen of England. The house contains a bizarre pedigree tracing Elizabeth's descent from Adam and Eve via Noah and King Lear.

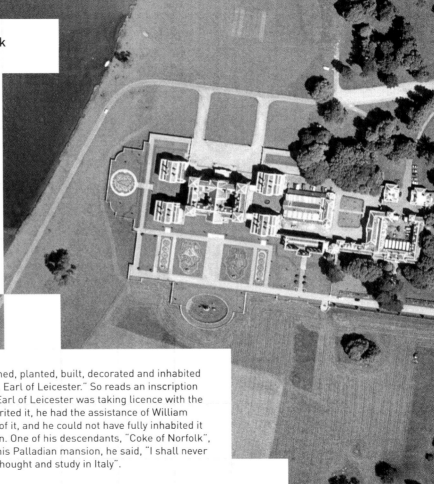

Holkham Hall
2 miles W of Wells-next-the-Sea, Norfolk

1. Built: 1734-59
2. Family: Coke, Earls of Leicester
3. Architect: Thomas Coke & William Kent
4. Built of: Yellowish brick
5. Features: Paintings by Rubens, Van Dyck, Gainsborough, Titian, Poussin
6. Other: The Hall houses the Bygones Museum in the stable block, with 5,000 items on display

Owner: Earl of Leicester
Tel: (01328) 710227

"This seat, on an open barren estate, was planned, planted, built, decorated and inhabited the middle of the XVIIIth century by Thos. Coke, Earl of Leicester." So reads an inscription inside the front door at Holkham Hall, but the Earl of Leicester was taking licence with the truth – the estate was not barren when he inherited it, he had the assistance of William Kent and the Earl of Burlington in the building of it, and he could not have fully inhabited it because he died five years before its completion. One of his descendants, "Coke of Norfolk", was more modest when, rather than altering this Palladian mansion, he said, "I shall never venture to interfere with the result of years of thought and study in Italy".

Ickworth

2.5 miles S of Bury St Edmunds, Suffolk

1. Built: 1795
2. Family: Earl of Bristol (also Bishop of Derry)
3. Architect: Mario Asprucci and the Sandys brothers
4. Built of: Brick faced with stone and stucco
5. Features: Paintings by Titian, Gainsborough, Velasquez, Hogarth, Reynolds; Pompeiian room by JD Crace
6. Gardens: Italianate garden; park designed by Capability Brown
7. Other: Ickworth was modelled on another circular house, Belle Isle on Lake Windermere

Owner: National Trust
Tel: (01284) 735270

This extraordinarily-shaped house at Ickworth was built to house the Earl-Bishop's vast art collection, which he described as "few pictures but choice ones". He intended "to have my galleries to exhibit an historical progress of the art of painting both in Germany and in Italy" but he was thwarted when in 1798 the French invaded Italy, occupied Rome and confiscated his collections.

Igtham Mote
2.5 miles S of Igtham, Kent

1. Built: 1340
2. Family: Cawne/de Haut/Selby
3. Architect: Additions by Cawne/Sir Richard Clement
4. Built of: Stone, timber and brick
5. Features: Great Hall, crypt and courtyard
6. Other: The name Mote comes not from moat but from the moot, or council, that met here in the Middle Ages

Owner: National Trust
Tel: (01723) 811145

According to legend Cromwell's soldiers set out to destroy Igtham Mote as a Royalist stronghold but they got lost in the deep wooded valleys surrounding the house and destroyed another building instead.

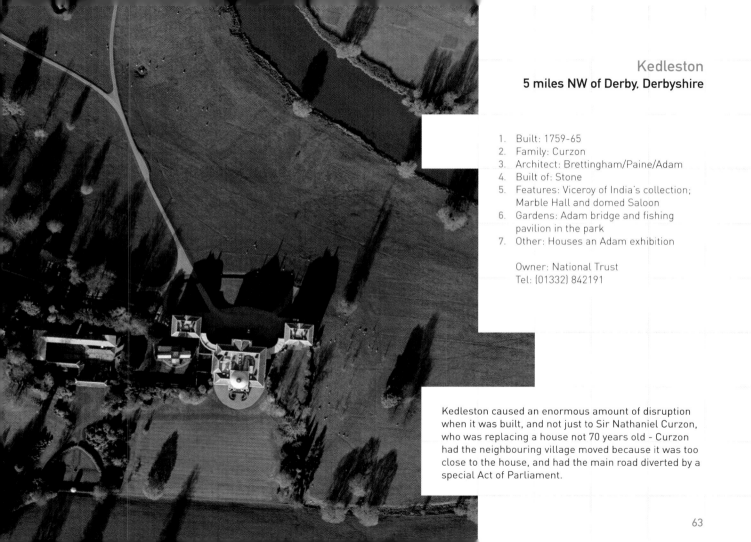

Kedleston
5 miles NW of Derby, Derbyshire

1. Built: 1759-65
2. Family: Curzon
3. Architect: Brettingham/Paine/Adam
4. Built of: Stone
5. Features: Viceroy of India's collection; Marble Hall and domed Saloon
6. Gardens: Adam bridge and fishing pavilion in the park
7. Other: Houses an Adam exhibition

Owner: National Trust
Tel: (01332) 842191

Kedleston caused an enormous amount of disruption when it was built, and not just to Sir Nathaniel Curzon, who was replacing a house not 70 years old - Curzon had the neighbouring village moved because it was too close to the house, and had the main road diverted by a special Act of Parliament.

Kensington Palace
London W8

1. Built: Jacobean/1689-90
2. Family: Crown
3. Architect: Remodelled by Wren & Hawksmoor
4. Built of: Brick
5. Features: Paintings by Tintoretto and Van Dyck; Royal Ceremonial Dress collection
6. Other: Birth of Queen Victoria, 24 May 1819; William and Mary bought what was then Nottingham House and had Wren convert it for them into Kensington Palace

Owner: Historic Royal Palaces
Tel: (020) 7376 2716

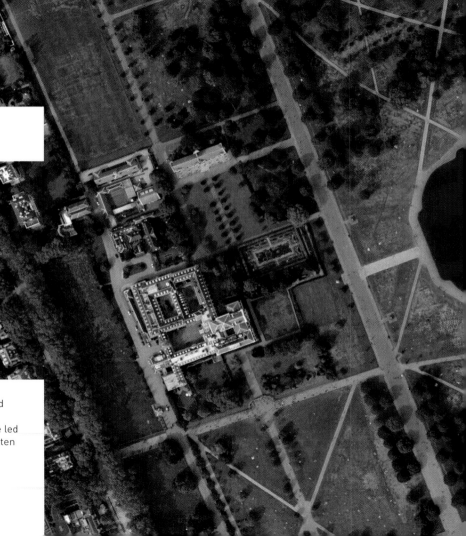

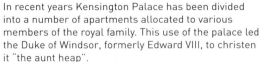

In recent years Kensington Palace has been divided into a number of apartments allocated to various members of the royal family. This use of the palace led the Duke of Windsor, formerly Edward VIII, to christen it "the aunt heap".

Kenwood
Hampstead, London NW3

1. Built: 17th century/1764-79
2. Family: Mansfield/Iveagh
3. Architect: Remodelled by Robert Adam, 18th century
4. Built of: Faced brick
5. Features: The Iveagh bequest, including paintings by Rembrandt, Vermeer, Turner, Gainsborough and Reynolds
6. Gardens: Wooded grounds laid out by the 1st Earl of Mansfield, 18th century
7. Other: Location for the films Notting Hill and Mansfield Park; Lord Iveagh, head of the Guinness family, bequeathed the house, contents and grounds to the nation in 1927

Owner: English Heritage
Tel: (020) 8348 1286

It is by two strokes of luck that Kenwood has survived for public view. Not only was it saved for the nation from developers by Lord Iveagh but it was almost ransacked by the Gordon rioters in 1780. The Earl of Mansfield was a deeply unpopular Attorney-General and Lord Chief Justice, having sent 102 people to the gallows and sentenced a further 448 to transportation. The rioters had already ransacked his Bloomsbury house and were making their way towards Kenwood when they were distracted en route by the landlord of the Spaniard's Inn, who happened to be an ex-butler of Mansfield's – he gave the rioters free drinks until soldiers arrived to break up the now-drunken mob.

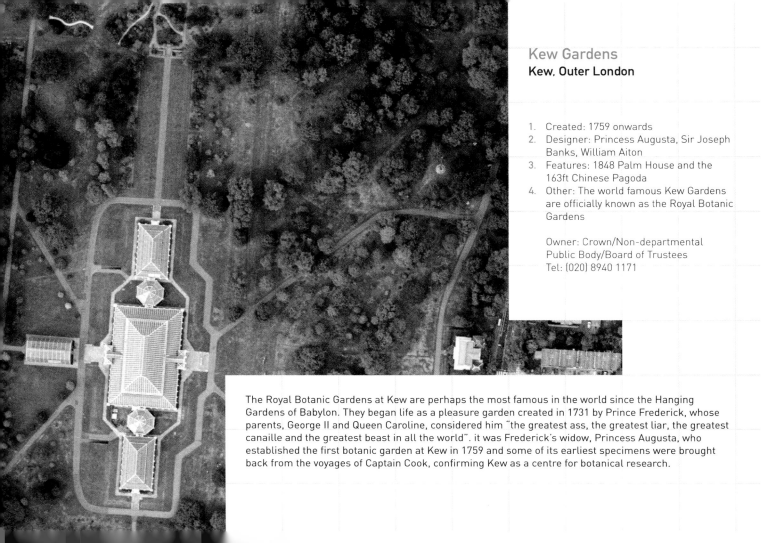

Kew Gardens
Kew, Outer London

1. Created: 1759 onwards
2. Designer: Princess Augusta, Sir Joseph Banks, William Aiton
3. Features: 1848 Palm House and the 163ft Chinese Pagoda
4. Other: The world famous Kew Gardens are officially known as the Royal Botanic Gardens

Owner: Crown/Non-departmental Public Body/Board of Trustees
Tel: (020) 8940 1171

The Royal Botanic Gardens at Kew are perhaps the most famous in the world since the Hanging Gardens of Babylon. They began life as a pleasure garden created in 1731 by Prince Frederick, whose parents, George II and Queen Caroline, considered him "the greatest ass, the greatest liar, the greatest canaille and the greatest beast in all the world". it was Frederick's widow, Princess Augusta, who established the first botanic garden at Kew in 1759 and some of its earliest specimens were brought back from the voyages of Captain Cook, confirming Kew as a centre for botanical research.

Knole
Sevenoaks, Kent

1. Built: 1456/1603
2. Family: Sackville, Earls & Dukes of Dorset
3. Architect: Thomas Bourchier/Thomas Sackville
4. Built of: Kentish ragstone
5. Features: Paintings by Van Dyck, Gainsborough, Reynolds, Lely, Kneller, Hoppner; prototype of the Knole settee
6. Other: Knole inspired Virginia Woolf's Orlando; said to be designed to numerically match the calendar, with 7 courtyards, 52 staircases and 365 rooms

Owner: National Trust
Tel: (01732) 462100

Thomas Bourchier transformed Knole House into a palace for himself and succeeding Archbishops of Canterbury but it was later appropriated by Henry VIII and then passed by Elizabeth I to Thomas Sackville. Vita Sackville-West wrote that Knole "has the deep inward gaiety of some very old woman who has always been beautiful, who has had many lovers and seen many generations come and go, smiled wisely over their sorrows and their joys and learnt an imperishable secret of tolerance and humour".

Lacock Abbey
3 miles S of Chippenham, Wiltshire

1. Built: 13thC/1540s
2. Family: Sharington/Talbot
3. Architect: Sir William Sharington
4. Built of: Stone
5. Features: 13th-century sacristy, chapter house and warming room
6. Gardens: Rare trees planted by William Henry Fox Talbot
7. Other: The first photographic negative, which featured the small oriel window in the South Gallery, was produced at Lacock by William Henry Fox Talbot, a descendant of Sharington

Owner: National Trust
Tel: (01249) 730227

The abbey has been lived in continuously since it was founded in 1232 by Ela, Countess of Salisbury, who was also the first Abbess. It was dissolved in 1539 and sold to Sir William Sharington, who preserved most of the medieval buildings and employed one of Henry VIII's stonemasons to convert the abbey into a residential house.

Lambeth Palace
London SE1

1. Built: c1200/1828-34
2. Family: Archbishops of Canterbury
3. Architect: For Archbishop Hubert Walter/restored by Edward Blore
4. Built of: Red brick
5. Features: Portraits of Archbishops by Holbein, Van Dyck, Hogarth, Reynolds; Tudor Gatehouse, 1486-1501 by Archbishop Morton
6. Other: John Wycliffe was tried in the chapel for heresy, 1378; attacked by rioters 1381 (Wat Tyler), 1640 (London apprentices) and 1780 (Gordon riots); official residence of the Archbishop of Canterbury; used as a prison during the Commonwealth

Owner: Church commissioners for England
Tel: (020) 7898 1200

In 1575 Archbishop Matthew Parker died at Lambeth Palace and was buried in the chapel. During his lifetime he was notorious for meddling in state affairs and he is thought to be the original "nosey Parker".

Lanhydrock
2.5 miles SE of Bodmin, Cornwall

1. Built: c1640/19th century
2. Family: Robartes
3. Architect: Robartes
4. Built of: Granite
5. Features: Louis XIV Boulle writing tables; Long Gallery showing Old Testament scenes
6. Gardens: Famous avenue of beeches and sycamores
7. Other: Sequestered by Royalists during the Civil War

Owner: National Trust
Tel: (01208) 73320

Lanhydrock was originally built as a foursquare mansion around a central courtyard but the east side was demolished in 1780, resulting in the present plan which was recreated after a fire in 1881 – only the north wing and the porch with its coat of arms survived the fire.

Levens Hall
5 miles S of Kendal, Cumbria

1. Built: 13th C/1570-1640
2. Family: Bellingham
3. Architect: additions by Col James Grahme
4. Built of: Local stone, slate roof
5. Features: Steam engine collection
6. Gardens: garden by Col James Grahme; Topiary garden by M Beaumont, 1694
7. Other: Location for the BBC's Wives & Daughters; Monsieur Beaumont was gardener to James II at Hampton Court

Owner: CH Bagot Esq
Tel: (01539) 560321

Levens Hall is an Elizabethan mansion built around a 13th century pele tower. Pele towers were built across northern England and Scotland in the Middle Ages as houses suitable for sudden defence against raiders, often having a vaulted chamber on the ground floor for cattle with the upper storeys for people.

Liverpool University Botanic Gardens
Ness Gardens, Ness-on-Wirral, Cheshire

1. Created: Founded 1898
2. Designer: Arthur Kilpin Bulley
3. Features: Tree and shrub collections,
   water and rock gardens, herbaceous
   borders and glasshouses
4. Other: The emphasis of the gardens is
   on research, conservation and public
   education.

Owner: Liverpool University
Tel: (0151) 353 0123

In 1898, Arthur Kilpin Bulley, a Liverpool cotton broker, founded Ness Gardens
by building his house on a gorse-covered sandstone outcrop overlooking the
Dee Estuary. He incorporated the surrounding fields into what has now become
one of the country's leading botanic gardens and on his behalf intrepid plant
collectors scoured the mountains of China and the Himalayas for alpine and
hardy plants which could be cultivated in this country. After his death the
Gardens were bequeathed to the University by his daughter Lois Bulley, in 1948.

Longleat House
Warminster, Wiltshire

1. Built: 1568-80
2. Family: Marquess of Bath
3. Architect: Sir John Thynne
4. Built of: Stone
5. Features: Titian's Holy Family; Bishop Ken's library with 30,000 books
6. Gardens: Designed by Capability Brown; now a safari park
7. Other: A chain of lakes forms the long leat, or watercourse, after which the house is named

Owner: Marquess of Bath
Tel: (01985) 844400

In 1946 Longleat became the first stately home to open to the paying public, and twenty years later Capability Brown's landscapes were transformed into the country's first drive-through safari park. Eclipsing the house itself, attractions now include the world's largest hedge maze, a Doctor Who exhibition and a high-tech simulation of the world's most dangerous modes of travel.

Loseley Park
2 miles SW of Guilford, Surrey

1. Built: 1562
2. Family: Molyneux
3. Architect: For Sir William Moore
4. Built of: Ragstone
5. Features: Family portrait by Van Somer; walled gardens
6. Other: Loseley House is built of greenish-grey ragstone from the ruins of Waverley Abbey

Owner: Michael More-Molyneux
Tel: (01483) 304440

The Walled Gardens at Loseley Park include a Herb Garden that illustrates the culinary, medicinal, dyeing and cosmetic uses of herbs.

Lyme Park
6.5m SE of Stockport, Cheshire

1. Built: 16th/18th C
2. Family: Legh
3. Architect: Giacomo Leoni/Lewis Wyatt
4. Built of: Stone
5. Features: Clock collection, carvings by Grinling Gibbons, ceilings by Francis Conseiglio and Joseph Polfreman
6. Other: Featured as Pemberley in the BBC's Pride and Prejudice

Owner: National Trust
Tel: (01663) 762023

Aside from its architecture and family connections, Lyme Park is also famous for the Lyme mastiff, a breed which died out in the 19th century. The house contains a copy of Velasquez's Las Meninas, which portrays a Lyme mastiff descended from one reared here and presented to Philip II of Spain in 1604.

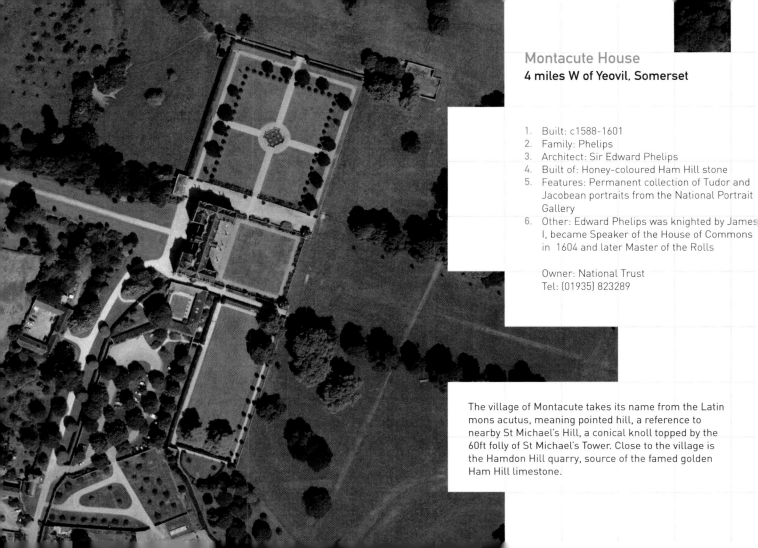

Montacute House
4 miles W of Yeovil, Somerset

1. Built: c1588-1601
2. Family: Phelips
3. Architect: Sir Edward Phelips
4. Built of: Honey-coloured Ham Hill stone
5. Features: Permanent collection of Tudor and Jacobean portraits from the National Portrait Gallery
6. Other: Edward Phelips was knighted by James I, became Speaker of the House of Commons in 1604 and later Master of the Rolls

Owner: National Trust
Tel: (01935) 823289

The village of Montacute takes its name from the Latin mons acutus, meaning pointed hill, a reference to nearby St Michael's Hill, a conical knoll topped by the 60ft folly of St Michael's Tower. Close to the village is the Hamdon Hill quarry, source of the famed golden Ham Hill limestone.

Moseley Old Hall
4 miles N of Wolverhampton, Staffordshire

1. Built: c1600
2. Family: Whitgreave
3. Architect: Henry Pitt
4. Built of: Timber-framed/brick
5. Features: Charles II's bed and hiding place; eaves chapel; knot garden
6. Other: Charles II sheltered here after the Battle of Worcester in 1651; in 1600 Moseley Old Hall was known as "Mr Pitt's new Hall at Moseley"

Owner: National Trust
Tel: (01902) 782808

After the Restoration, Charles II dictated to Samuel Pepys the story of how he had arrived at Moseley disguised as a woodcutter and sheltered there for two days and a night before making his escape to France. Cromwell's troops came to the house and questioned the owner Thomas Whitgreave but the King, crouching in one of Moseley's many priest-holes, remained undetected.

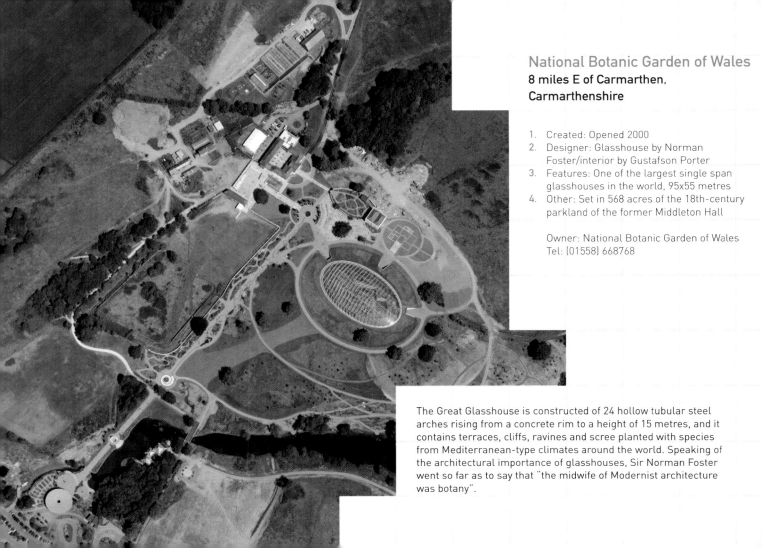

National Botanic Garden of Wales
8 miles E of Carmarthen, Carmarthenshire

1. Created: Opened 2000
2. Designer: Glasshouse by Norman Foster/interior by Gustafson Porter
3. Features: One of the largest single span glasshouses in the world, 95x55 metres
4. Other: Set in 568 acres of the 18th-century parkland of the former Middleton Hall

Owner: National Botanic Garden of Wales
Tel: (01558) 668768

The Great Glasshouse is constructed of 24 hollow tubular steel arches rising from a concrete rim to a height of 15 metres, and it contains terraces, cliffs, ravines and scree planted with species from Mediterranean-type climates around the world. Speaking of the architectural importance of glasshouses, Sir Norman Foster went so far as to say that "the midwife of Modernist architecture was botany".

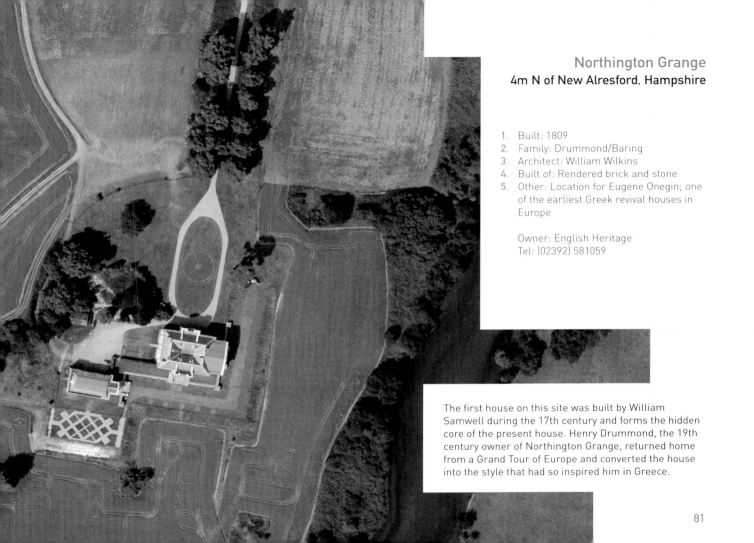

Northington Grange
4m N of New Alresford, Hampshire

1. Built: 1809
2. Family: Drummond/Baring
3. Architect: William Wilkins
4. Built of: Rendered brick and stone
5. Other: Location for Eugene Onegin; one of the earliest Greek revival houses in Europe

Owner: English Heritage
Tel: (02392) 581059

The first house on this site was built by William Samwell during the 17th century and forms the hidden core of the present house. Henry Drummond, the 19th century owner of Northington Grange, returned home from a Grand Tour of Europe and converted the house into the style that had so inspired him in Greece.

Nostell Priory

6 miles SE of Wakefield, West Yorkshire

1. Built: Mid-18th century
2. Family connection: Winn
3. Architect: James Paine/Robert Adam
4. Built of: Stone
5. Features: Chippendale furniture; plasterwork by Joseph Rose, ceilings by Zucchi and Kauffmann
6. Other: The famous Nostell doll's house is thought to be the earliest extant work of Thomas Chippendale

Owner: National Trust
Tel: (01924) 863892

A longcase clock at Nostell still keeps perfect time after nearly 300 years. It was made in 1717 by John Harrison, the son of the estate carpenter, who went on to solve the problem of longitude by inventing the chronometer. The house also contains furniture by Thomas Chippendale who was born just a few miles away at Otley and received his training from the Harrisons.

Osborne House
1 mile SE of Cowes, Isle of Wight

1. Built: 1845-51
2. Family: Crown
3. Architect: Prince Albert/Thomas Cubitt
4. Built of: Brick rendered to look like Bath stone
5. Features: Victoria's furniture and personal effects
6. Other: Death of Queen Victoria, 1901; the grounds contain the Swiss Cottage, built as a playhouse for the royal children

Owner: English Heritage
Tel: (01983) 200022

Queen Victoria wrote of Osborne that "it is impossible to imagine a prettier spot. Valleys and woods which would be beautiful anywhere; but all this near the sea is quite perfection."

Osterley Park House
Osterley, Middlesex

1. Built: 1575/1761-80
2. Family: Gresham/Child
3. Architect: Robert Adam (18th century)
4. Built of: Brick
5. Features: Gobelin tapestry
6. Gardens: 140 hectares of park and farmland
7. Other: Sir Thomas Gresham was financial advisor to Elizabeth I and founder of the Royal Exchange

Owner: National Trust
Tel: (020) 8232 5050

Osterley Park might never have become open to public view were it not for the fact that Sarah Anne Child eloped to Gretna Green with the Earl of Westmoreland in 1782 and thereby lost her inheritance. The Child fortune, including Osterley Park, went instead to her younger sister Sophia, who married the Earl of Jersey in 1804 – their descendant the 9th Earl gave the property to the National Trust in 1949.

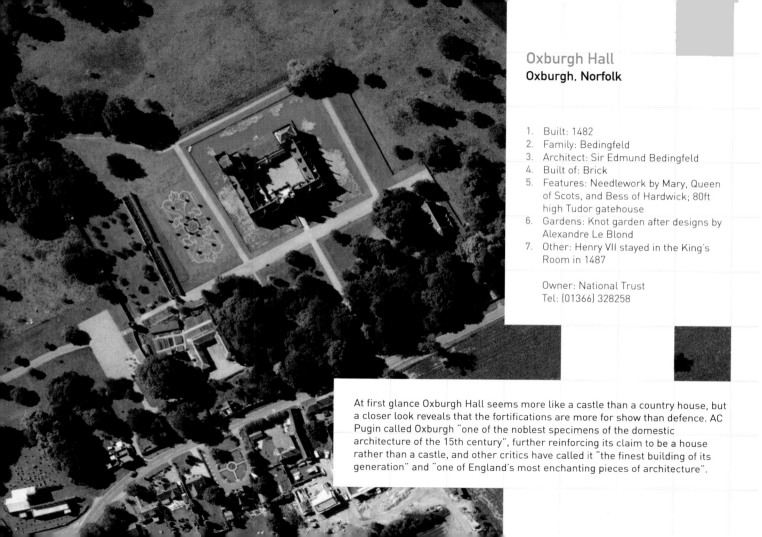

Oxburgh Hall
Oxburgh, Norfolk

1. Built: 1482
2. Family: Bedingfeld
3. Architect: Sir Edmund Bedingfeld
4. Built of: Brick
5. Features: Needlework by Mary, Queen of Scots, and Bess of Hardwick; 80ft high Tudor gatehouse
6. Gardens: Knot garden after designs by Alexandre Le Blond
7. Other: Henry VII stayed in the King's Room in 1487

Owner: National Trust
Tel: (01366) 328258

At first glance Oxburgh Hall seems more like a castle than a country house, but a closer look reveals that the fortifications are more for show than defence. AC Pugin called Oxburgh "one of the noblest specimens of the domestic architecture of the 15th century", further reinforcing its claim to be a house rather than a castle, and other critics have called it "the finest building of its generation" and "one of England's most enchanting pieces of architecture".

Packwood House
2 miles E of Hockley Heath, Warwickshire

1. Built: 1556-60/20th century
2. Family: Fetherston
3. Architect: William Fetherston/Graham Baron Ash
4. Built of: Staffordshire brick
5. Features: Collection of tapestries and textiles; George I walnut chairs
6. Gardens: The allegorical topiary garden, representing the Sermon on the Mount, is thought to be by John Fetherston, c1655

Owner: National Trust
Tel: (01684) 855362

Packwood is famous for its topiary garden and herbaceous borders, and even the garden walls have unusual features – one has a row of "bee-holes" designed to hold bee skeps, another has internal hot water pipes to provide an outdoor greenhouse, with peach trees growing along the wall.

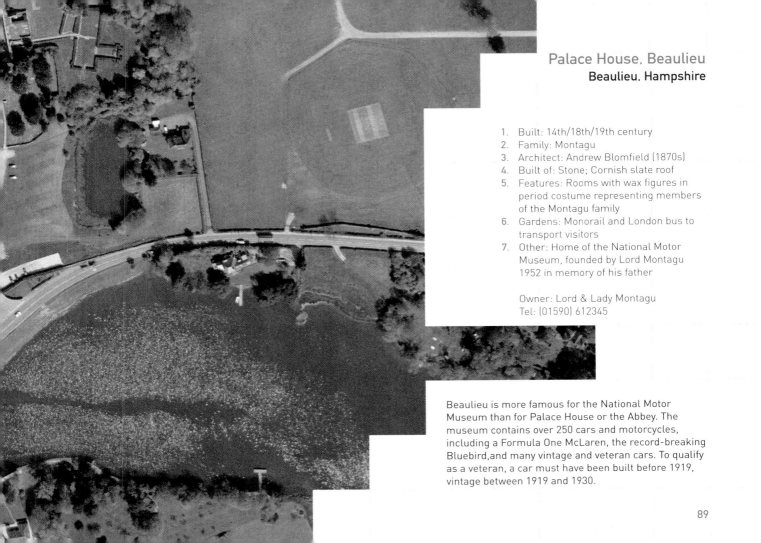

Palace House, Beaulieu
Beaulieu, Hampshire

1. Built: 14th/18th/19th century
2. Family: Montagu
3. Architect: Andrew Blomfield (1870s)
4. Built of: Stone; Cornish slate roof
5. Features: Rooms with wax figures in period costume representing members of the Montagu family
6. Gardens: Monorail and London bus to transport visitors
7. Other: Home of the National Motor Museum, founded by Lord Montagu 1952 in memory of his father

Owner: Lord & Lady Montagu
Tel: (01590) 612345

Beaulieu is more famous for the National Motor Museum than for Palace House or the Abbey. The museum contains over 250 cars and motorcycles, including a Formula One McLaren, the record-breaking Bluebird, and many vintage and veteran cars. To qualify as a veteran, a car must have been built before 1919, vintage between 1919 and 1930.

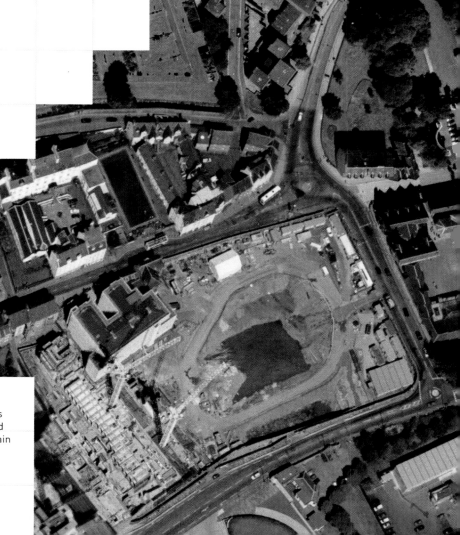

Palace of Holyroodhouse
Edinburgh, Midlothian

1. Built: 16th-17th century
2. Family: Crown
3. Architect: For James IV and later Charles II
4. Built of: Stone
5. Features: Great Gallery with 89 portraits by Jacob de Wet of Scottish monarchs; 17th century state rooms
6. Other: Mary, Queen of Scots held court here from 1561-67; murder of David Rizzio in 1566; the Young Pretender's 1745 banquet here is described in detail in Walter Scott's novel Waverley; official Scottish residence of the British royal family

Owner: Crown
Tel: (0131) 556 1096

The original Palace developed out of the royal guest house of the Abbey of Holyrood, founded by David I as "a house for Canons devoted to the Cross" – Holyrood means holy cross. It was rebuilt for James IV and again for Charles II, whose south-west tower mirrors the north-west tower built for his great-great-great-grandfather more than 150 years earlier.

Petworth House
Petworth, West Sussex

1. Built: 1688-96
2. Family: Percy/Dukes of Somerset/Wyndham
3. Architect: 6th Duke of Somerset
4. Built of: Local freestone ashlar, Portland stone
5. Features: Paintings by Turner, Gainsborough, Rembrandt, Van Dyck, Blake, Bosch; Grinling Gibbons room; murals by Louis Laguerre
6. Gardens: Designed by Capability Brown, 1751-57
7. Other: The 6th Duke of Somerset was known as The Proud Duke because of his obsessive arrogance

Owner: National Trust
Tel: (01798) 342207

Petworth is as famous for its paintings as its architecture, in particular the series of Turners inspired by Capability Brown's park and lake. The 3rd Earl of Egremont was a renowned patron of British artists, and Turner was his favourite guest – modern visitors can stand beside Turner's view of the park from the house, and by looking out of the window see the painting repeated.

Philipps House & Dinton Park
9 miles W of Salisbury, Wiltshire

1. Built: 1816
2. Family: Wyndham/Philipps
3. Architect: Jeffry Wyatt
4. Built of: Stone
5. Features: Ionic portico on south façade
6. Gardens: 48 hectares by the Wyndham family, 18th century
7. Other: The architect, Jeffry Wyatt (nephew of James Wyatt), later became known as Sir Jeffry Wyatville

Owner: National Trust
Tel: (01985) 843600

The Wyndhams bought the estate at Dinton in the late 17th century and built the present house close to where their earlier family home then stood. In 1917 the family sold the estate to Bertram Philipps, after whom the house is now named.

Polesden Lacey
2 miles S of Great Bookham, Surrey

1. Built: 1823/1906
2. Family: Greville
3. Architect: Thomas Cubitt
4. Built of: Stucco on brick
5. Features: Dutch, Italian and Flemish paintings and portraits by Richardson, Reynolds, Lawrence and Raeburn
6. Gardens: 1,000 acres; walled garden by Mrs Greville, with her tomb at the entrance
7. Other: George VI and Queen Elizabeth, now The Queen Mother, spent part of their honeymoon here when they were Duke & Duchess of York

Owner: National Trust
Tel: (01372) 458203

In 1797 the dramatist Sheridan bought a house on the site of Polesden Lacey, and wrote to his wife: "I have every hour a new reason to be pleased with our purchase – we shall have the nicest place, within prudent distance of town, in England."

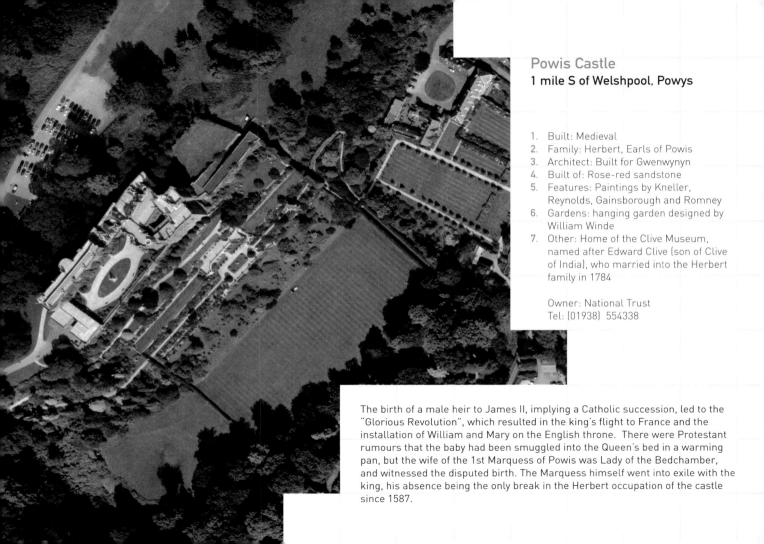

Powis Castle
1 mile S of Welshpool, Powys

1. Built: Medieval
2. Family: Herbert, Earls of Powis
3. Architect: Built for Gwenwynyn
4. Built of: Rose-red sandstone
5. Features: Paintings by Kneller, Reynolds, Gainsborough and Romney
6. Gardens: hanging garden designed by William Winde
7. Other: Home of the Clive Museum, named after Edward Clive (son of Clive of India), who married into the Herbert family in 1784

Owner: National Trust
Tel: (01938) 554338

The birth of a male heir to James II, implying a Catholic succession, led to the "Glorious Revolution", which resulted in the king's flight to France and the installation of William and Mary on the English throne. There were Protestant rumours that the baby had been smuggled into the Queen's bed in a warming pan, but the wife of the 1st Marquess of Powis was Lady of the Bedchamber, and witnessed the disputed birth. The Marquess himself went into exile with the king, his absence being the only break in the Herbert occupation of the castle since 1587.

Queen's House
Greenwich, London SE10

1. Built: 1616-38
2. Family: Crown
3. Architect: Inigo Jones
4. Built of: Rendered brick, Portland stone
5. Features: Iron open-well Tulip staircase
6. Other: Originally the house straddled the main Deptford-Woolwich road, giving access to both the park and river

Owner: National Maritime Museum
Tel: (020) 8312 6602

Queen's House, "a perfect Palladian villa", was commissioned in 1616 by Anne of Denmark, the queen of James I, but she died in 1619 and building stopped until Inigo Jones was asked to complete it for Charles I's queen, Henrietta Maria. She was so pleased with Queen's House that it became known as "The House of Delights".

Ragley Hall
1.5 miles SW of Alcester, Warwickshire

1. Built: 1679-1683
2. Family: Seymour
3. Architect: Robert Hooke/ additions by James Wyatt
4. Built of: Brick and stone
5. Features: Plasterwork by James Gibbs, mural by Graham Rust (The Temptation of Christ)
6. Gardens: 400 acres by Capability Brown; 8000 acres of farm- and woodland

Owner: Lord and Lady Hertford
Tel: (01789) 762090

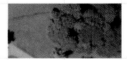

In 1743 the Rev Jeremiah Milles, on a visit from Ireland, described "Ragley house" as being "a noble seat... upon an eminence commanding a most noble prospect of ye country round about".

Rosemoor RHS Garden
1m SE of Great Torrington, Devon

1. Created: Presented to RHS 1987
2. Designer: Lady Anne Palmer (later Berry)
3. Features: 200 varieties of rose; herb garden, potager, winter garden, alpine terrace, herbaceous borders
4. Other: The Royal Horticultural Society's first Regional Garden and second in importance to Wisley

Owner: Royal Horticultural Society
Tel: (01805) 624067

Originally used as a fishing lodge on the west-facing slopes of the Torridge Valley, the Rosemoor estate covers 40 acres and, apart from a few exotic trees around Rosemoor House, most of the garden has been created since 1970. The Visitor's Centre was opened in 1990 to the west of the road that bisects the garden, and the planting since then is beginning to mature in sympathy with Lady Anne's Garden on the other side of the road. After presenting Rosemoor to the RHS, Lady Anne Palmer moved to New Zealand, where she set up the Hackfalls Arboretum.

Rousham House
Rousham, Oxon

1. Built: 1635
2. Family connection: For Sir Robert Dormer
3. Architect: William Kent
4. Built of: Stone
5. Features: Interiors by William Kent 1738
6. Gardens: William Kent
7. Other: Used as a Royalist garrison in the Civil War; Alexander Pope was a friend of the Dormer brothers

Ownership: C Cottrell-Dormer Esq
Tel: (01869) 347110

Horace Walpole described Rousham Park as the most engaging of all William Kent's landscape creations, calling it the most "elegant and antique". Kent also built a sham castle gate on the hill, a folly now known as the "Rousham eyecatcher".

Royal Pavilion
Brighton, East Sussex

1. Built: 1815-22
2. Family: Prince Regent (later George IV)
3. Architect: Henry Holland/John Nash
4. Built of: Cast iron domes
5. Features: One-tonne chandelier hung from the jaws of a dragon on the ceiling of the Banqueting Room
6. Other: New techniques in cast iron made the domes and minarets possible

Owner: Brighton and Hove City Council
Tel: (01273) 290900

"The dome of St Paul's must have come to Brighton and pupped"; "Coleridge's pleasure-dome transported from Xanadu to an English seaside resort." Two comments, made 150 years apart, which both highlight the fact that the Royal Pavilion, with its domes, pinnacles and minarets, looks somewhat out of place in Brighton – and yet Brighton wouldn't be Brighton without it. Once a royal palace built for the Prince Regent, Queen Victoria was not amused by the Royal Pavilion and sold it to the town since when it has been used as a tearoom, hospital, concert hall, radar station and ration office, but has now been restored.

St Michael's Mount
0.5 miles S of Marazion, Cornwall

1. Built: Medieval
2. Family: Crown/Cecil/St Leven
3. Architect: Additions by St Aubyn
4. Built of: Granite
5. Features: Rococo Gothic drawing room
6. Other: Perkin Warbeck was imprisoned here in the late 1490s; St Michael is supposed to have appeared here in 495, after which the mount was considered sacred

Owner: National Trust (partly owned by Lord St Leven)
Tel: (01736) 710507

Milton described "the great vision of the guarded mount", which according to Arthurian legend is part of the lost kingdom of Lyonesse. Deep inside the mount itself is a vaulted cell carved into the rock, reached by a tight spiral staircase that emerges under a pew in the choir of the church.

Saltram House
2 miles W of Plympton, Devon

1. Built: 1743-50
2. Family: Parker
3. Architect: John Parker
4. Built of: Stucco
5. Features: Painting by Reynolds and Angelica Kauffmann; Robert Adam saloon and dining room; ceilings by Rose and Zucchi
6. Gardens: 202 hectare park laid out by Richmond in the style of Capability Brown
7. Other: John Parker II was a close friend of Joshua Reynolds, and bred a Derby winner called Saltram

Owner: National Trust
Tel: (01752) 336546

The 18th century novelist Francis Burney wrote of Saltram in 1789 that "the house is one of the most magnificent in the kingdom, its view is noble". There is a small temple in the garden overlooking the Plym estuary, a view no longer quite so noble, which is known as Fanny's Bower in her honour.

Sandringham House
Sandringham, Norfolk

1. Built: 1869-70
2. Family connection: Crown (built for Edward VII)
3. Architect: AJ Humbert
4. Built of: Red brick and Bath stone
5. Features: Tapestries woven from Goya cartoons, a gift from the King of Spain
6. Gardens: 60 acres around house, 7,000 acre estate
7. Other: Haunted by a page boy; Sandringham museum (Royal memorabilia); Queen Alexandra's dogs are buried in the grounds

Owner: Crown
Tel: (01553) 772675

King George V wrote "Dear old Sandringham, the place I love better than anywhere else in the world". High praise indeed.

Sandy RSPB Nature Reserve
1 mile E of Sandy, Bedfordshire

1. Created: Acquired by RSPB 1961
2. Designer: Acquired by Secretary Philip Brown
3. Features: Specialist widlife garden created in conjunction with the Henry Doubleday Association
4. Other: Headquarters of the Royal Society for the Protection of Birds

   Owner: RSPB
   Tel: (01767) 680541

The nature reserve consists of managed woodland and heathland and supports a wide variety of birds and wildlife, including woodpeckers, nuthatches, tits and finches. The formal and wildlife gardens, run by organic methods, are also open to the public, with nature trails of up to 5.6 km (3½ miles).

Shugborough Estate
6m E of Stafford, Staffordshire

1. Built: 18th century
2. Family: Anson, Earls of Lichfield
3. Architect: Altered by Samuel Wyatt 1790-1806
4. Built of: Part-stuccoed
5. Features: County Museum in stable block; rococo plasterwork by Vassalli
6. Other: The 1st Earl of Lichfield was Postmaster-General when the Penny Post was introduced

Owner: National Trust
Tel: (01889) 881388

The fortune that allowed Thomas Anson to create Shugborough came in large part from Spanish treasure. Anson's younger brother George, Admiral Anson the Circumnavigator, had returned to England with a large share of spoils that included the capture of the annual Spanish trans-Pacific galleon and its cargo worth £400,000.

Stanford Hall
1.5 miles from Swinford, Leicestershire

1. Built: 1697
2. Family: Cave
3. Architect: William Smith of Warwick
4. Built of: Brick, with stone south façade
5. Features: Hepplewhite and Queen Anne furniture
6. Other: Aviation museum in the stables commemorating Percy Pilcher, who crashed in the grounds

Owner: The Lady Braye
Tel: (01788) 860250

Stanford Hall was built for Sir Roger Cave and has remained in the family for over three hundred years since – he was an ancestor of the present owner, the Lady Braye. The village of Swinford lies in the Vale of the White Horse, home to the poets William Morris, Dante Gabriel Rossetti, Alexander Pope and Matthew Arnold, and to novelist Thomas Hughes, who wrote about the area in Tom Brown's Schooldays.

Stourhead
Stourton, Wiltshire

1. Built: 1721
2. Family: Hoare
3. Architect: Colen Campbell
4. Built of: Doulting stone
5. Features: Chippendale furniture; Angelica Kauffmann paintings
6. Gardens: Laid out 1741-1780 by Henry Hoare
7. Other: In the grounds stands the 50m high King Alfred's Tower, a red brick folly by Henry Flitcroft, 1772

Owner: National Trust
Tel: (01747) 841152

The gardens at Stourhead include a lake formed by damming the Stour, Temples to Flora and Apollo, a Grotto dedicated to the Nymphs of the Grot, and the Pantheon, which houses Michael Rysbrack's Hercules. In 1762, Horace Walpole described the gardens as "one of the most picturesque scenes in the world".

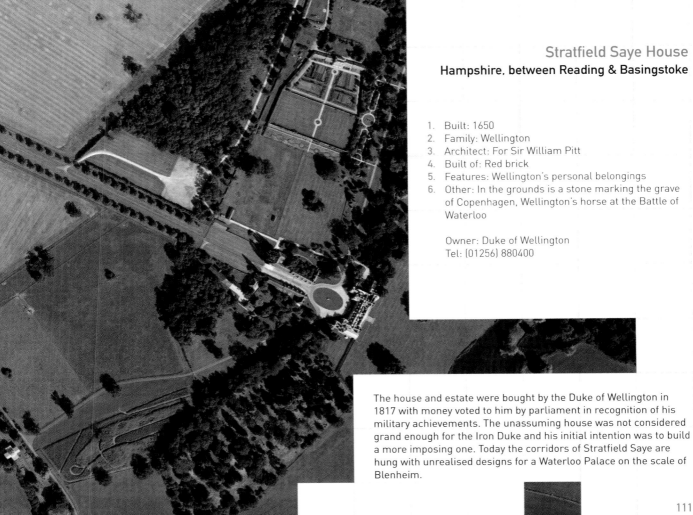

Stratfield Saye House
Hampshire, between Reading & Basingstoke

1. Built: 1650
2. Family: Wellington
3. Architect: For Sir William Pitt
4. Built of: Red brick
5. Features: Wellington's personal belongings
6. Other: In the grounds is a stone marking the grave of Copenhagen, Wellington's horse at the Battle of Waterloo

Owner: Duke of Wellington
Tel: (01256) 880400

The house and estate were bought by the Duke of Wellington in 1817 with money voted to him by parliament in recognition of his military achievements. The unassuming house was not considered grand enough for the Iron Duke and his initial intention was to build a more imposing one. Today the corridors of Stratfield Saye are hung with unrealised designs for a Waterloo Palace on the scale of Blenheim.

111

Sudeley Castle
Winchcombe, Gloucestershire

1. Built: 1442/restored 1830
2. Family: Seymour/Dent
3. Architect: For Ralph Boteler
4. Built of: Stone
5. Features: Paintings by Turner, Constable; Catherine Parr is buried in Chapel; rose collection in the Queen's Garden
6. Other: Held by Royalist Lord Chandos during the Civil War; haunted by a Victorian servant; in 1469 Boteler was forced to sell the castle to the future Richard III; used as Prince Rupert's HQ during the Civil War

   Owner: Lord and Lady Ashcombe
   Tel: (01242) 602308

Henry VIII, Anne Boleyn, Lady Jane Grey and Elizabeth I all stayed at Sudeley Castle, although it was never a royal residence. Catherine Parr, Henry VIII's 6th wife, came to live here after her marriage to Thomas Seymour, Lord of Sudeley, following the king's death.

Tatton Park
2 miles N of Knutsford, Cheshire

1. Built: 19th century
2. Family: Egerton
3. Architect: Samuel Wyatt/Lewis Wyatt
4. Built of: Faced with yellow brick
5. Features: Egerton collection and Gillow furniture; Japanese garden with Shinto temple
6. Gardens: Designed by Humphry Repton and Sir Joseph Paxton
7. Other: Tenant's Hall houses the 4th Lord Egerton's trophies, including a tiger shot when Egerton was 81

Owner: National Trust
Tel: (01625) 534400

Samuel Wyatt, architect of Tatton Park, died in 1807 before it was finished. His work was completed by his nephew Lewis, who also added an orangery, conservatories, and a triumphal arch at the Knutsford entrance.

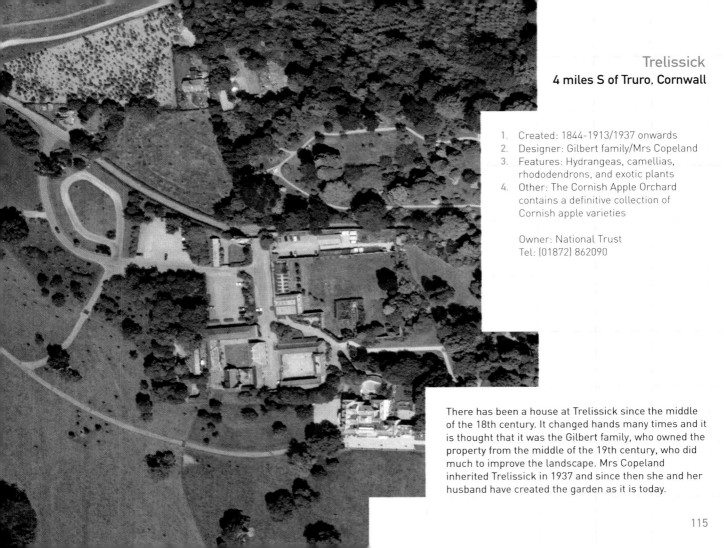

Trelissick
4 miles S of Truro, Cornwall

1. Created: 1844-1913/1937 onwards
2. Designer: Gilbert family/Mrs Copeland
3. Features: Hydrangeas, camellias, rhododendrons, and exotic plants
4. Other: The Cornish Apple Orchard contains a definitive collection of Cornish apple varieties

Owner: National Trust
Tel: (01872) 862090

There has been a house at Trelissick since the middle of the 18th century. It changed hands many times and it is thought that it was the Gilbert family, who owned the property from the middle of the 19th century, who did much to improve the landscape. Mrs Copeland inherited Trelissick in 1937 and since then she and her husband have created the garden as it is today.

Trengwainton
2 miles W of Penzance, Cornwall

1. Created: 1814/1925-69
2. Designer: Sir Rose Price/Sir Edward Bolitho
3. Features: A series of square walled enclosures with raised terrace beds, planted with magnolias and rare conifers, and underplanted with shrubs and plants normally seen under glass
4. Other: Three types of rhododendron flowered at Trengwainton for the first time in England

Owner: National Trust
Tel: (01736) 363021

Sir Rose Price was the son of a wealthy Jamaican sugar planter and he established the garden at Trengwainton early in the 19th century by planting hardwood trees around the house and creating the distinctive brick-walled gardens. After his death the estate was sold and later inherited by Lt-Col Edward Bolitho, who participated in Kingdon Ward's 1927-28 botanical expedition to Assam and Burma. The greater part of Trengwainton's renowned collection of rhododendrons derives from seeds brought back from the expedition.

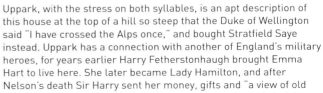

Uppark

1.5 miles S of South Harting, West Sussex

1. Built: 17th century
2. Family: Forde/Fetherstonhaugh
3. Architect: William Talman/additions by Repton
4. Built of: Brick and stone
5. Features: Fetherstonhaugh collection of paintings and decorative art
6. Gardens: Grounds by Humphry Repton, who charged a fee of 50 guineas per visit
7. Other: Partially destroyed by fire on 30th August 1989; HG Wells spent his early years here – his mother became housekeeper in 1880

Owner: National Trust
Tel: (01730) 825415

Uppark, with the stress on both syllables, is an apt description of this house at the top of a hill so steep that the Duke of Wellington said "I have crossed the Alps once," and bought Stratfield Saye instead. Uppark has a connection with another of England's military heroes, for years earlier Harry Fetherstonhaugh brought Emma Hart to live here. She later became Lady Hamilton, and after Nelson's death Sir Harry sent her money, gifts and "a view of old Uppark dans la belle saison".

Waddesdon Manor

6 miles NW of Aylesbury, Buckinghamshire

1. Built: 1874-89
2. Family: Rothschild
3. Architect: GH Destailleur
4. Built of: Bath stone
5. Features: Paintings by Gainsborough and Reynolds; wine cellars with 15,000 bottles of Rothschild wine
6. Other: A special railway line was built to carry the Bath stone to the site on land bought from the Duke of Marlborough

Owner: National Trust
Tel: (01296) 653226

Waddesdon Manor was owned by the Rothschilds, a family whose renown prompted one wit to say that "to be a Rothschild horse or dog was considered an enviable distinction among more plebeian quadrupeds". Lord Rothschild's cows were said to eat out of silver mangers, and his brother Alfred was in the habit of riding in a pony-cart pulled by zebras.

Wakehurst Place
1.5 miles NW of Ardingly, West Sussex

1. Created: 1903
2. Designer: Gerald WE Loder/Sir Henry Price
3. Features: Woodland and lakes, with a Winter Garden, Rock Walk and "Bloomer's Valley"
4. Other: Administered by the Royal Botanical Garden at Kew

Owner: National Trust
Tel: (01444) 894066

The Sussex Weald is ideal for the creation of gardens, with its retentive acid soil, varied terrain, and wooded slopes and valleys. For these reasons the area is home to many famous gardens but Wakehurst has been variously described as "the most beautiful", "the most spectacular", and "the most unusual".

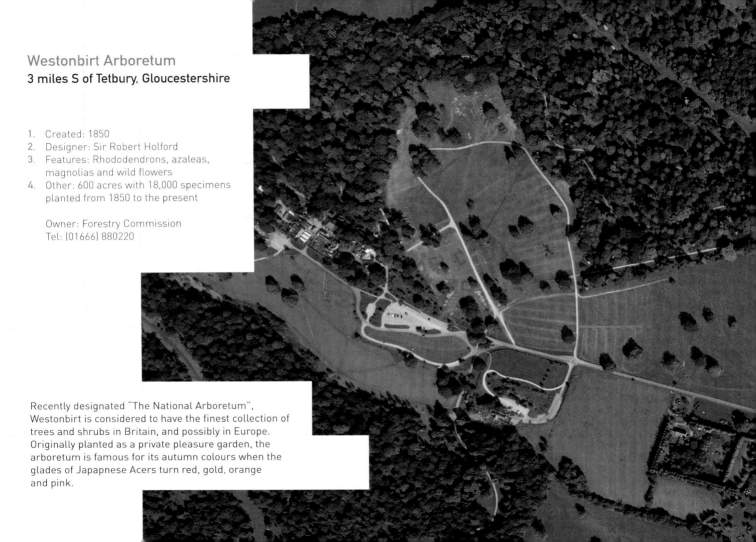

Westonbirt Arboretum
3 miles S of Tetbury, Gloucestershire

1. Created: 1850
2. Designer: Sir Robert Holford
3. Features: Rhododendrons, azaleas, magnolias and wild flowers
4. Other: 600 acres with 18,000 specimens planted from 1850 to the present

   Owner: Forestry Commission
   Tel: (01666) 880220

Recently designated "The National Arboretum", Westonbirt is considered to have the finest collection of trees and shrubs in Britain, and possibly in Europe. Originally planted as a private pleasure garden, the arboretum is famous for its autumn colours when the glades of Japapnese Acers turn red, gold, orange and pink.

Wilton House
3 miles W of Salisbury, Wiltshire

1. Built: Tudor/1647
2. Family: Herbert, Earls of Pembroke
3. Architect: William Herbert/Inigo Jones and John Webb
4. Built of: Stone
5. Features: Paintings by Van Dyck, Rembrandt; furniture by Chippendale and William Kent; Single and Double Cube rooms by Inigo Jones
6. Gardens: 21 acres including the famous Palladian bridge
7. Other: Rebuilt after a fire in 1647; As You Like It thought to have been first performed here; Philip Sidney wrote part of Arcadia here; Jonson and Donne visited

Owner: Earl of Pembroke
Tel: (01722) 746720

Daniel Defoe wrote that "One cannot be said to have seen anything that a man of curiosity would think worth seeing in this country and not have been at Wilton House".

Winkworth Arboretum
2 miles SE of Godalming, Surrey

1. Created: Presented to the National Trust in 1932
2. Designer: Dr Wilfrid Fox
3. Features: 96 acres with two lakes and views over the North Downs
4. Other: Winkworth is the National Trust's only true arboretum

Owner: National Trust
Tel: (01483) 208477

Sixty acres of the current ninety-six were presented to the National Trust by Dr Wilfrid Fox, who devoted years of his time to nurturing the previously neglected woodland. Winkworth is renowned for the splendour of its autumn colours, which are said to "rival the glory of an American fall".

Wisley RHS Garden
Woking, Surrey

1. Created: presented to the RHS 1903
2. Designer: Sir Thomas Hanbury
3. Features: The Garden of the Senses was opened in 1998, containing the RHS's first major collection of Bonsai.
4. Other: Wisley is the flagship of the RHS, described as "a working encyclopaedia for gardeners of all levels".

Owner: Royal Horticultural Society
Tel: (01483) 211113

The garden's creator, Sir Thomas Hanbury, was a renowned gardener and philanthropist, having made his fortune as a merchant in Shanghai where he planted public gardens and campaigned against slavery and opium. After returning to Europe he created the famous botanic gardens at La Mortola, endowed the Genoa Botanical Institute, created public gardens at Ventimiglia and Alassio, and bought the then 60 acre estate at Wisley and presented it to the Royal Horticultural Society.

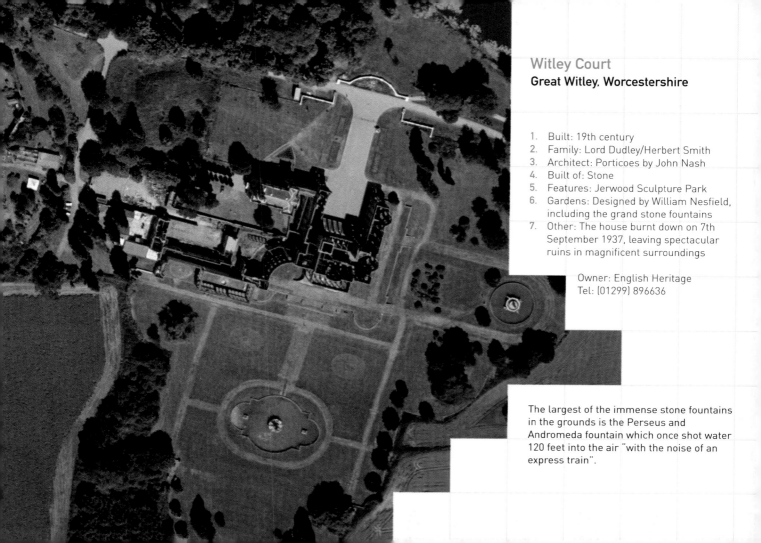

Witley Court
Great Witley, Worcestershire

1. Built: 19th century
2. Family: Lord Dudley/Herbert Smith
3. Architect: Porticoes by John Nash
4. Built of: Stone
5. Features: Jerwood Sculpture Park
6. Gardens: Designed by William Nesfield, including the grand stone fountains
7. Other: The house burnt down on 7th September 1937, leaving spectacular ruins in magnificent surroundings

Owner: English Heritage
Tel: (01299) 896636

The largest of the immense stone fountains in the grounds is the Perseus and Andromeda fountain which once shot water 120 feet into the air "with the noise of an express train".

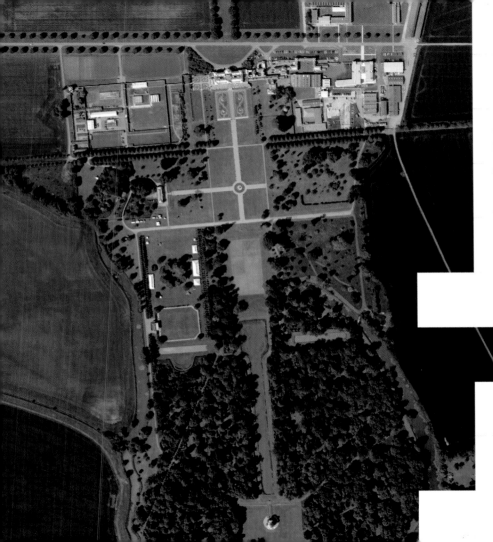

Wrest Park Gardens
0.75 miles E of Silsoe, Bedfordshire

1. Created: Early 18th/mid 19th century
2. Designer: Duke of Kent/Capability Brown
3. Features: The Archer Pavilion, which has chambers decorated with wall paintings
4. Other: Buildings and follies including a Mithraic Altar, Bowling Green House and a Chinese temple and bridge

Owner: English Heritage
Tel: (01525) 860152

The New House at Wrest Park was built for the de Grey family from 1834-39 and forms an elegant backdrop to the gardens. The formal 19th century gardens are beautifully complemented by the Long Water in front of the house, and provide a contrast with the earlier woodlands.

First published in 2001 by
HarperCollinsPublishers
77–85 Fulham Palace Road
London W6 8JB

The HarperCollins website address is:
www.fireandwater.com

Photography © 2001 Getmapping plc

Getmapping plc hereby asserts its moral right to be identified as the author
of this work.

Getmapping can produce an individual print of any area shown in this book,
or of any area within the United Kingdom. The image can be centred
wherever you choose, printed at any size from A6 to 7.5 metres square, and
at any scale up to 1:1,000. For further information, please contact
Getmapping on 01530 835685, or log on to www.getmapping.com

A CIP catalogue record for this book is available from the British Library.

ISBN: 0 00 711570 9

05 04 03 02 01
9 8 7 6 5 4 3 2 1

Text by Ian Harrison
Design by Colin Brown
Photographic image processing by Getmapping plc
Colour origination by Digital Imaging
Printed and bound by Bath Press Colourbooks